# A Little Book of Pendulum Magic

D. J. Conway

CROSSING PRESS
Berkeley | Toronto

**Library of Congress Cataloging-in-Publication Data**

Conway, D.J. (Deanna J.)
  A little book of pendulum magic / D.J. Conway.
     p. cm.
  Includes bibliographical references.
  1. Fortune-telling by pendulum.  I. Title

BF1779.P45 C66 2001
133.3—dc21                                          2001017461

ISBN-13: 978-1-58091-093-4 (pbk.)

Printed in the United States of America

Cover design by Victoria May
Cover photo by Nathan Walker
Interior design by Karen Narita

19  18  17  16  15  14  13  12
First Edition

# Contents

# Illustrations

# Foreword

Oh, the magic of pendulums! Swaying, mesmerizing, delighting us in their cosmic glory. Who hasn't sat entranced by the gentle sway of Grandfather's clock? What heart doesn't soften at a locket moving across a young mother's breast as her infant daughter gazes upon the moonbeams reflected there?

Pendulums and their compelling motion are all around, deliciously enticing us to partake of their wonderful energy. Here, in *A Little Book of Pendulum Magic*, they sneak up and grab us full force with power and magic and the wonders of motion and artistry.

D. J. Conway explores pendulums and the forces they employ in a manner that leaves one unable to look at the clock or the mother's necklace the same way again. What magic lies there? What answers? Life often flashes by us, half-formed. To grasp the wonder of the pendulum is to find fruition of life, to control, to enhance, to fulfill it with fun and deftly opened right brain activity. For eight thousand years or more humans have implemented the mysteries of pendulum power. Chapter by chapter, Conway's book teaches and sharpens the skills and the senses necessary to willfully and enchantingly use that power. You will learn to choose, build, use, and become one with the sway of the positive vibrations contained there; and you will become enchanted as well as the enchanter.

Here lies the past, the present, the future. Here is magic. Here is one of the greatest cosmic forces ever to be grasped by humankind. *A Little Book of Pendulum Magic* is your handbook. Use it wisely, safely, and lovingly.

Devon Cathlin
*B.A., Religion and the Wiccan Ministry*
*Certified Tarot Master*

# CHAPTER 1

# The History of Pendulums

Dowsing, or divining, for everything from water to precious metals to future events has an extremely long history of use by humankind. The words "dowsing" and "divining" have exactly the same meaning: to use a rod or pendulum to find something. The art of dowsing may have begun with the ancient shamans who needed to provide water for their clans. Later, this talent passed to the more structured religious classes who used it for finding water or metals, discovering the causes of illness, or divining the future.

The oldest record of dowsing being used by humans may be the pictographs on the walls of the Tassili Caves in south Algeria. Dating from about 6,000 B.C.E., these paintings show stylized human figures holding forked sticks.

The wand, or rod, is probably the most ancient of all divining instruments. Some writers of dowsing history cite the biblical reference of Moses finding water within a rock with his wand or staff. Today, however, the wand is not as popular as pendulums, L-rods, or forked twigs for divination or finding underground water or other objects.

Pendulums of all kinds are mentioned in the very oldest written records of divination and the occult arts. Ancient Chinese records tell of a ring suspended on a silk thread that was used to predict the future and warn of danger. The Chinese emperor Yu, who lived during 2,000 B.C.E., was said to be a dowser.

Predicting the future was often perilous to the health of the diviner. Although ancient Rome used divination of all kinds, usually the bloody entrails type, there are records before 400 B.C.E. of Roman diviners being executed for using a pendulum for this purpose, usually in an attempt to use the information against the Roman government.

One such case, recorded by Ammianus Marcellinus (c. 325–392 C.E.), explains a condemnation and execution that occurred because the diviners were using the information gained in just such a manner. Marcellinus was a noble Greek by birth and also a Roman historian. He told of a group of Roman conspirators during the first century C.E. who plotted the assassination of a man who would succeed the Roman emperor. In order to know who this next emperor would be, they suspended a ring on a thread from a tripod over a circle with alphabet letters around the edge. Using the pendulum like a

Ouija board, the conspirators learned the man's name. Before they could carry out the assassination, they were arrested and condemned.

Another account from ancient Rome tells of a pendulum being used in another manner similar to the Ouija board. In this case, a round pendulum was held inside a glass. The user slowly recited the alphabet letters. When the correct letter was said, the pendulum tapped against the side of the glass.

The use of various tools for dowsing continued through the centuries without much negative comment or repercussions until the Middle Ages. Then it came under attack by the Christian Church.

Pope John XXII issued a bull in 1326 C.E. that directly attacked the use of the pendulum or any other dowsing tool used for any purpose whatsoever. The Pope and the Vatican claimed that the pendulum-wielding diviner got the answers straight from the Devil. This edict led to other restrictions, which brought about the persecutions and burnings of so-called Witches during the Burning Times of the Inquisition in the Middle Ages and the Renaissance. Some figures for these murders estimate that nine million people were killed. Since many of the victims were the village midwives, healers, and dowsers, the Church termed them all Witches and Pagans and executed them. The last Witch was killed in Calvinist Scotland in 1728 C.E.

Martine de Bertereau, a Frenchman who lived during the mid-1600s, was a highly successful dowser for coal mines. In fact, he found one hundred fifty such mines before he was condemned by the Church and imprisoned for life. However, good dowsers for water, coal, and metal were so important to the existence of communities that it was impossible for the Church to suppress them all. The townspeople were not about to turn any dowser over for execution and lose their economic edge.

After the persecutions stopped, pendulums and other dowsing tools were used more openly. However, for a long time they doubled as tools of a guild trade, which curtailed suspicion. An example of this, which still survives today, is the carpenter's plumb bob. There is a science museum in South Kensington, London that has a unique collection of tools used by the guilds in the seventeenth and early eighteenth centuries. Among these items is an engraving of two men holding dowsing rods and a third man with a large pendulum.

Scientific investigations of the pendulum were carefully conducted as far back as the late 1700s. One such investigator was Johann Wilhelm Ritter, known as the father of electrochemistry. He performed many tests with the pendulum and was soundly ridiculed by his colleagues for dabbling in "superstitious nonsense." However, Ritter proved through his experiments that the pendulum could provide answers to anything by connecting with the collective unconscious (superconscious or universal mind), as Carl Jung called it. Ritter's detailed studies interested other noted researchers including Professor Antoine Gerboin of the University of Strasbourg, who went so far as to publish a book of two hundred fifty-three tests for using the pendulum.

This book, in turn, influenced Michel-Eugene Chevreul, who gave twenty years of his life to studying the pendulum. Chevreul was a director of the Natural History Museum in Paris in 1830. Chevreul, like Ritter before him, determined that there was a direct connection between the subconscious and superconscious minds of the user and the movement of the pendulum. Today, the pendulum is still sometimes called Chevreul's pendulum.

In the mid-1920s, a Major Pogson of Britain was dowsing for water for the Bombay Government, under British rule. He was greatly successful at this, even when more orthodox methods had turned up nothing. He became the official Water Diviner and visited all the districts of Bombay seeking underground water. One official report on his work states that Major Pogson found water in two hundred twenty of the five hundred seventy-seven sites he dowsed and never failed when he predicted water at a certain depth.

Evelyn Penrose, who was born in Cornwall, was hired by the government of British Columbia in 1931 to find water and minerals. Having an astounding success rate of 90 percent, Penrose was considered to be a valuable employee.

During the 1930s and early 1940s, a clergyman by the name of Abbé Alexis Mermet helped many people in France and Switzerland by finding water and healing people. He also helped the police find missing people. He had a very high success rate. Mermet believed that his clairvoyant powers, combined with a pendulum and a map, enabled him to trace a missing person. He frequently used map dowsing to locate these lost people, but he also came up with accurate details that had nothing to do with maps.

A woman asked him to help her locate her missing brother. The police had gotten nowhere. She provided Abbé Mermet with a photo of the young man that he held in one hand while using the pendulum over a map with the other. Keeping his questions to ones that could be answered Yes or No, the Abbé determined that the brother was dead. He described where the body could be found, how he had been killed, a general description of the man who did it, and why. The police found the body exactly where the Abbé said it would be, with a knife wound in the heart. His empty purse was discovered nearby in the River Sarine. The brother had obviously been the victim of a robbery.

After World War I, Abbé Mermet used his map dowsing to help the French government locate unexploded German shells. Although a few hundred years earlier Abbé Mermet would have been burned at the stake by the Church, the Vatican recognized him for his work in May, 1935. He invented a special type of pendulum made of several different metals, the top of which could be unscrewed and tiny samples of the sought material placed inside. This is still known as the Mermet pendulum and can be purchased at many New Age bookstores.

Dowsers and diviners are still working today in various areas of the world. Bill Lewis from Wales has worked with Paul Devereux on The Dragon Project, where he found radioactivity at the Rollright Stone Circle. Another dowser, Fran Farrelly from Florida, has worked with Stanford Research International in Menlo Park, California.

Today, the pendulum is once more becoming a popular tool for dowsing, healing, and gaining insight into future events. The pendulum is the most versatile and popular of all divining instruments. However, it is also the one most misused and misunderstood. Its simplicity easily lends itself to use by those who have no self-discipline to learn the craft correctly. Although not everyone will become as proficient as Major Pogson or Abbé Mermet with a pendulum, with practice, patience, and persistence, anyone can learn to use this divining tool.

# CHAPTER 2

# Making and Using a Pendulum

$P$endulums have become very popular in the last few years. There appears to be an inborn human fascination with this divination and dowsing tool that spans cultural backgrounds and ethnic origins.

However, many people give up using a pendulum when they don't get immediate results or seem to get ambiguous answers. Pendulums do work if used properly, but it takes practice, patience, persistence, and experience before one can distinguish between nonsense answers and the truth. After all, you are creating a link with your subconscious mind, which only speaks and understands symbols and symbolic reasoning. If you get the signals wrong, the subconscious mind will not know how to answer other questions. It will become confused. It is up to the pendulum user to develop the skills needed to correctly interpret the coded language of her/his subconscious mind.

The world today is basically geared to the left-brain or analytical and linear thinking. In fact, this "rational" side of our brain and lives is overfed. Schools and businesses rarely try to emphasize the right-brain or creative, intuitive abilities. We are taught to analyze everything, but follow orders without question. It is almost like walking around all the time with one closed eye and one deaf ear. Our subjective, intuitive, right-brain is starving. In order for pendulum divining to work properly, you have to learn to let go with the left-brain and allow the right-brain the freedom to bring up answers.

One of the easiest ways to learn to access the right-brain is through the practice of meditation. This quiet activity allows the creative side of the brain to get exercised, especially if one does not practice the Eastern idea of "no thought," but instead lets the mind cast up whatever mental pictures and expressions it wishes. Meditation is a backdoor method of strengthening the intuitive side of the brain and thus the intuition itself. Other easy methods of right-brain stimulation are the use of the pendulum, tarot cards, runes, or other divination tools. By presenting the left-brain with a physical object to consider, one can create an unobstructed avenue for the right-brain to cast up intuitive messages.

Intuition and dowsing are so closely connected that they may be one and the same thing. One thing is certain, however, the practice of dowsing will exercise your intuitive thinking, thereby causing you to become more aware of nudges from the psychic areas of your mind.

Herbert Weaver, in his book *Divining, the Primary Sense*, did experiments that led him to believe that the dowser or diviner responds to electromagnetic fields given off by the object sought. This definition of electromagnetic fields is a scientific way of describing what psychic people call vibrations. Everything has an energy field that forms an aura around the person, animal, or object. These auras or energy fields vibrate, even in inanimate objects. It is this vibration that is felt and "read" by psychics and dowsers.

Dowsing, like everything else in this world, is not 100 percent accurate. We are dealing with intuition and the collective unconscious sending messages through a human mind. No matter how highly skilled in whatever profession, no human is correct all the time. This fact is even more pertinent when working with intuitive, subconscious messages. Every impression and subconscious message has the possibility of being analyzed, interpreted, and censored by the left-brain. Beginners in anything make a lot of mistakes, and pendulum divining is no exception. However, anyone who is sensitive, and this includes a large percentage of people, can get a reaction from and learn to use a pendulum or dowsing rods.

Dowsers rarely do well in scientific tests of any kind. Perhaps this is because those critical of the practice remove everything intuitive and subjective and insist that only the linear be used. Scientists are notorious for disbelieving anything that cannot be seen, touched, cut up, or made to move a dial. So it is best not to engage in any test with a disbeliever. The only person you need to prove anything to is yourself.

Since you cannot learn to dowse or divine with a pendulum by reading about it, I suggest you make or buy a pendulum before you go any further in this book. Then practice each exercise as you read through the book. Although the exercises require more than a cursory attempt if you want to become proficient and get reliable answers to your questions, you can learn to get movement results from a pendulum almost immediately.

Technically, a pendulum is any balanced weight hung on a thread or string. This can be a cork with a darning needle run through the exact center, a hexagonal nut on a string, a carpenter's plumb bob, or, according to folk tradition, a wedding ring suspended on a hair. Although these makeshift pendulums will work if you have nothing else to use, only the carpenter's plumb bob is very effective. The others are either too light in weight or their shape is not conducive to good movement. Although traditionally it is possible to make a pendulum out of rings, buttons, corks, or pencils, these do not prove to be very accurate pendulums. They are far too light and unbalanced. A pencil with a needle stuck in the eraser may be heavier and more balanced, but its long, thin shape is not the best for a pendulum, particularly for beginners.

One of the easiest pendulums to make uses a natural quartz crystal point. Glue a bail to the top and thread a string through the bail. The pendulum is ready to use as soon as it is dry. The crystal point, however, must not have any rough debris on the sides or it will not hang properly.

Another quickly made pendulum is a man-made crystal drop found in many stores. Although you can thread a string directly through the hole in the top of the drop, it makes a better pendulum if you attach a large jump-ring first, then thread the string through the ring. Thread attached directly to the top of a pendulum has a tendency to slip one way or the other, thus throwing the pendulum off balance.

Another inexpensive type of homemade pendulum is a lead fishing weight. Purchase a lead sinker weighing from 1/2 ounce to 2 ounces. Tie about 10 inches of lightweight nylon fishing line to the top of the weight. Begin with about 3 inches of line hanging between the lead weight and your fingers. Gently swing the line, increasing the hanging length as necessary, until you find the point where the weight swings easily and freely. This is the proper length for using the lead sinker as a pendulum.

Some people prefer the bullet-type pendulum, which is a 1-inch steel weight about the thickness of a pencil and pointed at one end. This shape vaguely mimics the many natural crystal points offered in many New Age shops. Although some purists try to dissuade people from buying pendulums shaped by craftsmen in this fashion or man-made crystals, I have not found any difficulty using either type.

Other shapes for pendulums are the fat, little, round ones with a point, or those shaped entirely like a ball. The round pendulums with a shaped point at the bottom are usually made of brass, bronze, or a combination of metals, such as the Mermet pendulum mentioned in chapter 1. Other ball pendulums are frequently made of wood, plastic, man-made crystal, or various types of shaped natural stone. Many dowsers do not like round, ball-shaped pendulums. However, one of my most responsive pendulums is a round, plastic one on a cheap chain.

Whatever you decide to use as a pendulum, do not use one that is so light it has no weight to swing or so heavy that your hand quickly becomes tired. Although any shape of pendulum that is properly balanced will work for most questions, a pointed pendulum is best to use for map dowsing, particularly if you are using the pendulum itself instead of a pointer to indicate specific areas on the map.

You can tell if the pendulum weight and shape is appropriate for you by the length of time it takes the pendulum to swing or move. If it moves very slowly or not at all, try varying the length of the string. Then check to see if the pendulum is balanced exactly at the center. If these changes do not correct the problem, try a pendulum that is heavier, lighter, or differently shaped. The least effective type of pendulum shape for most people, particularly for beginners, is one that is long and thin, like a pencil.

Pendulums are readily available in rock shops and New Age stores, or from any pagan supplier. When purchasing a pendulum, always choose one that feels good to you. Everyone is familiar with the unexplainable feeling that something is not quite right about a car, a house, a computer, or a piece of jewelry. This feeling frequently manifests by an uncomfortable feeling in the pit of your stomach. It is your psychic sensing or gut feeling warning you that the object in question is not right for you. You can better sense this feeling from a pendulum if you hold it cupped between your hands. The negative vibrations of a pendulum may range from prickly to slimy. No matter how good the price or how much you want a pendulum made of a certain stone, it is not to your benefit to purchase one that makes you the slightest uneasy.

When a pendulum is good for you, it will make you feel

comfortable with it. Its vibrations may be cold, hot, tingly, or pulsating, depending upon the material from which it is made.

Next, test the way the pendulum is balanced and weighted by dangling it from its string. Is the weight heavy enough to be felt through the string or chain? If it is too light, the pendulum will be affected by the slightest of movements, whether of your hand or the air. You need to select a pendulum that weighs from 1/2 ounce to 2 ounces. Each person's requirements will be different.

Is the pendulum bail or hole centered, and is the pendulum shaped properly? If the bail or hole is off-center, the pendulum will not respond properly. If a string is tied directly to the pendulum, I suggest that you attach a small jump-ring through the hole in the top of the pendulum and retie the string to the jump-ring. If the pendulum does not have a hole through the top, which would be unusual, you need to purchase a bail and glue it on. String directly tied to the pendulum has the habit of slipping to one side or the other and throwing off the hanging balance of your device.

Some pendulums, particularly those carved out of stone, may not be shaped symmetrically. The shape may be heavier or thicker on one side than on the other, or the hole at the top may be off-center. If the pendulum shape is good but the hole not centered, you can correct this by gluing a bail to replace the hole. However, there is nothing you can do about a badly shaped pendulum.

Eventually you may acquire a collection of pendulums of different shapes, materials, and sizes. It is best not to become dependent upon only one pendulum. You may find that some of your pendulums will not work properly or at all on certain types of questions. I have one pendulum made of lapis lazuli that refuses to answer questions unless they are of a spiritual nature. I did not choose this pendulum for that kind of questions and at first could not understand why it sometimes refused to move. When I began to pay attention, it became obvious that it was attuned to spiritual problems, not material ones.

A short list of stones and their traditional meanings is at the end of this chapter to help if you are planning to use stone energy in pendulum divining.

Purists also quibble over whether the pendulum should be suspended on a thread, string, or thin chain. Folk tradition states that it should be hung on a human hair, which actually does not make a good suspending thread at all. It is difficult to get a hair long enough, or strong enough, or flexible enough to tie the hair to the pendulum bail. Hair also frequently breaks. Thread is usually thin and strong, and is easily acquired. If you use string, it must not be too thick and should be strong and very flexible; a cheap string that breaks or frays easily is not a good choice. A very fine, short, silver neck chain makes a good suspending thread if it is flexible. A chain with heavy links will not allow the pendulum to move freely. Try each kind until you find what works best with your pendulum. Also, what works well on one pendulum may not work smoothly on another one.

You will not need any great length of thread or chain for your pendulum, although it should be long enough so that you can adjust it if necessary. Hanging lengths of 6 to 8 inches usually work best. A pendulum that hangs down too far when you hold it will only get in your way. Each pendulum, depending upon its weight, will require a different length of thread.

The first thing you should do after purchasing a pendulum is to clean it of the vibrations left by anyone who handled it. You can easily do this by holding it under cool, running water if it is made of stone, gemstone, glass, or metal. If it is a wooden or cork pendulum, rub it gently between your hands until it warms with your vibrations. You can embed more of your vibrations into your pendulum by using it regularly.

When you find yourself without your pendulum in times of emergency, you can substitute a large button or metal nut on a string, or a needle with thread stuck into the eraser end of a short pencil. However, these are more difficult to use and can be far less accurate for a novice diviner.

The proper method for holding a pendulum is to grasp the suspending thread between your thumb and forefinger. Some people hold the string over the first joint of the forefinger, but this makes the string length keep changing and the finger is frequently in the way of the pendulum swing. The fingertips are very sensitive. Through them you can tell what the pendulum is doing without looking at it. Greater ease of movement is attained by holding the string between the thumb and forefinger.

The proper body position for working with a pendulum is important. Rest your elbow on a table and hold your grasping fingers so that they point downward. Do not cross your feet. Take several deep, slow, calming breaths. Most important, do not use the pendulum when you are tired or when you are ill at ease with another person or the questions she/he wants answered.

When you first begin using the pendulum for answering questions, start with only about 2 inches of thread hanging down between your fingers and the pendulum. Do not hold the pendulum thread too tight. If you do, this tension will keep the pendulum from moving freely. Gradually extend the length of string until the pendulum swings freely and easily for its weight. Some pendulum users recommend putting a knot in the string at this point, but I do not. The length needed for a good pendulum swing may vary from time to time, so a knot would only cause confusion. I have noticed that barometer changes and moon phases sometimes alter the length of thread needed.

When first working with a pendulum, or when you return to pendulum divining after a period of time, you need to practice on movements only. Leave the asking of questions until you become more proficient and confident with the pendulum.

To become good with a pendulum you need to practice a series of exercises for three to six weeks. Practice each of the exercises in this book in their order for the best results. This is to ensure that you understand each area of pendulum dowsing.

The first set of exercises consists of learning to make the pendulum move without any questions or motives behind it. By practicing these exercises you will learn that you can use the power of your subconscious mind to move your pendulum. This exercise helps you learn the difference in feeling between a true subconscious answer and an answer that is what you want. This also is the first step in communicating with the right-brain for dowsing.

Holding your pendulum in the above-described position, mentally tell the pendulum to make clockwise circles. Continue thinking this command at the pendulum until it circles in a clockwise direction (Figure 1, page 105). If the pendulum does not move, and your choice of a pendulum seems to be right for you, physically and gently cause the pendulum to move in the direction you wish it to go. Stop the pendulum, and again give it the mental command to circle clockwise. When you are successful in this, command the pendulum to stop. Repeat this exercise as many times as you need.

When you can control the pendulum through the circle and stop movements, work until you can command the pendulum to make first bigger, then smaller clockwise circles.

When you have mastered this exercise, practice counterclockwise circles (Figure 2, page 106). Tell the pendulum to stop. Proceed to making bigger and smaller counterclockwise circles. When you are successful with this, move on to forward and backward movements (Figure 3, page 107), then side-to-side movements (Figure 4, 108), ending each motion with the command to stop.

Commanding the pendulum to make specific movements may seem rather silly at first. However, these exercises make you aware of the difference in the feel of "commanded" movement and the motion that is spontaneous and will give a true answer. When you are commanding the pendulum, you have a pushy sensation just under your ribs, as you do when moving to swing higher in a swing. When you aren't mentally commanding the pendulum, you get a "floaty" or non-caring feeling. This is the best description I can give for the two different sensations.

When asking a question, you want your pendulum to give you a strong answer so there is no way you can wonder whether it is answering the question or simply being in the Neutral/Search mode. A friend gave me a statement given to her by her aunt: "Answers should be statements, not whispers or apologies." A true answer will not be a halfhearted pendulum movement, but a motion with strength.

Learning to command the pendulum is also essential as you must learn to stop the pendulum after one answer, before you go on to another question. Your subconscious mind needs to learn that when you issue a command to stop, the pendulum must stop, or when you mentally phrase a question, it must give the pendulum the correct answer.

If you experience difficulties in getting movement out of your pendulum, you may be too tense and trying too hard. Relax for a few moments before returning to the exercises. If this does not solve the problem, become aware of your body to see if you are too tired to be using the pendulum at that time. Also check the question itself, for you may not want to know the answer.

There is no one set of correct movements from a pendulum

to indicate an answer. Pendulums react differently to different people. The first position or movement of the pendulum you must identify is what is called the Neutral or Search position (Figure 5, page 109). This position should appear when the pendulum is merely hanging there waiting for you to give it a question. The pendulum may react in one of three different motions. It may hang still with no movement. It may show that it is in the Neutral/Search position by making very small clockwise circles. Or, it may gently swing side to side or forward and backward in short, tiny, straight movements. In order for the pendulum to establish a Neutral/Search position, you must tell it to stop. With a little practice, the pendulum will obey this command by hanging dead still or making a small movement. You need to know what movement your pendulum makes for a Neutral/Search answer so you can distinguish between a Neutral and a definite No or Yes answer.

Next, you must establish the Yes movement of your pendulum. Hold the pendulum in the proper position and ask it to show you a Yes movement (Figure 6, page 110). It will do this by either swinging sharply forward and backward or in a clockwise circle. After it has shown you the Yes movement, again ask it to stop.

Now you need to establish a No movement. When asked to show this, the pendulum will move either in a sharp side-to-side motion or a counterclockwise circle (Figure 7, page 111). After it has established the No movement, ask it to stop.

The Confusion or Wrong Question movement is either a left or right diagonal movement (Figure 8, page 112). This movement can also mean, "I don't know what to answer" or "This question can't be answered." It is important to know this movement, as it will occur whenever your question is not clear, you are confused about the question yourself, or you are approaching the situation with the wrong question.

If your Yes movement is forward and backward and your No movement side-to-side, the pendulum may divide the Confusion response by using a clockwise circle for a Maybe answer and a counterclockwise circle for a "This question cannot be answered" response.

You need to practice the Yes, No, Confusion, and Neutral movements with your pendulum once or twice a day for a minimum of three weeks before you begin to ask questions. This practice is necessary for setting up a symbolic code with your subconscious mind. Without this set symbolic code, you cannot get trustworthy answers. In fact, the pendulum may refuse to move at all or will give you nonsense answers.

Generally, the movements will be the same for all your pendulums, but on occasion you will find a pendulum that will not respond in the usual manner. Therefore, it is very important that you discover which movements mean what before you begin working.

Sometimes the code appears to become embedded in the pendulum itself by the person who uses it. In cases such as this, if another person uses the pendulum, it will not respond if the expected movements are different from the new user's code.

When you do move on to asking questions, keep in mind that you should never concentrate on the answer you want the pendulum to give because you will not get a truthful answer if you do. Instead, try to keep an expectant attitude, such as "I wonder what the answer will be?" The questions must be phrased in such a way that the only answers will be Yes or No. You cannot ask a pendulum "either-or" questions.

You should respect very standard ethics. Do not lower yourself to using the pendulum to snoop on another person or harm her/him in any way. The private lives of others are none of your business. You should not use your pendulum to pry into the affairs of others, no more than you would open their mail or tap their telephone lines. The same ethics apply if another person wants you to ask your pendulum such questions.

With Yes and No answers to questions, it is easy to work your way through a series of questions until you get the proper and sometimes unforeseen answers to the question you wish answered. Never expect a particular answer, or you will not get the truth. By asking a series of questions, you can determine whether it is the right question to ask, the correct solution you are seeking, or whether your goal is something you should abandon. Timing also plays an important part in pendulum divining, just as it does in the use of any foretelling method. Things, people, and events may not all be in place to give you the answer about a future event at that time.

Also being aware of the strength with which the pendulum answers questions will aid you in determining the validity of a question. A wide swing for Yes is unquestionable, while a half-hearted, weak swing means you could push the issue for which you ask, but it may not be worth the effort and you may not get a truthful answer. Dowsers must keep in touch with reality at all times or things will go wrong, and we will get the results we want instead of the truth. Therefore, you must be aware all the time and word questions very carefully.

Yes and No swings of a pendulum can also be used to answer such polarity questions as masculine and feminine, up and down, or hot and cold. The masculine/feminine polarity can be used to divine the sex of an unborn child or the sex of a person in a future event. For example, if you are considering a change in jobs, you might wish to ask if your new boss will be a man or a woman. The up and down description will help you when dowsing for lost objects. The hot and cold polarity is also useful when searching for something. Hot will mean you are closer to the object, while cold means you are going the wrong way.

Every dowser or diviner has periods when she/he seems to get nothing but idiot answers from her/his device. This frequently shows up when you are showing off instead of taking the pendulum and its powers seriously. This also may happen if the user is tired or uncomfortable asking the question. It may occur at other times for no known reason. This infrequent reaction seems to fall under the universal law that we can never have anything under control 100 percent of the time. When this happens, try another pendulum. If you still get idiot answers, it may be wise not to use the pendulum for a few days, until whatever universal energy affecting your pendulum has passed.

Easy exercises to try out your pendulum involve two and three coins. These simple exercises will help you gain confidence, satisfy your need to work with your pendulum, and aid you in gaining skill and understanding of pendulum movements.

First, take two coins of the same date and denomination. Place them on a table about your hand's length apart. Hold the pendulum in the correct position between these coins.

Ask the pendulum to point out the similar coins. Asking this sounds rather dim, I know, but you need the experience of seeing how your pendulum reacts (Figure 9, page 113). The pendulum either will swing back and forth between the two coins, or will oscillate in a clockwise circle over both coins.

Next, take three coins, two with the same date and denomination, the third one different. This may mean two coins of the same date, with a third of a different date, or two coins of the same denomination and the third of a different denomination. Place them on a table in a triangular pattern with about a hand's length between all the coins. Now ask the pendulum to show you which coins are the same. The pendulum will swing between the two identical coins (Figure 10, page 114).

Since working with a pendulum enhances your psychic senses, you should use the pendulum only for serious reasons, such as for the well being of other people and yourself, or genuinely to seek knowledge and truth in a situation. Never use a pendulum to show off or because you want others to think you are wonderful and talented. Life has a way of deflating one's ego in crushing and often embarrassing events.

When a pendulum ceases to be a curiosity or toy, you can use it as a valuable tool in your everyday life. You can test the quality of water or food, search out the basis for an allergy or illness, discover the right car for you before purchasing a vehicle, and locate lost objects or people. It can even lead you to diagnose elusive problems in car engines and other mechanical devices, locate the studs in a house wall, and trace underground pipes of various kinds.

You can use a pendulum to answer any question as long as the answer can be Yes or No. You can test foods, vitamins, herbs, or medicines to see if they will be good for you. To do this, hold a sample of the material being tested in one hand while you operate the pendulum with the other. There is more on this in chapter 4. However, never second-guess a prescribed medication. Always discuss such questions with your doctor.

After working with a pendulum for a period of time, you will notice that it frequently works better on some days than others. Do not be discouraged by this. The pendulum is reacting to your physical and emotional energy levels. These energy levels fluctuate during each day and from day to day. If the pendulum persists in not operating properly after several tries during a day, put it away until another time. Also check to see if you are too tense, as this will interfere with your success. It is never wise to practice more than fifteen minutes on any day. The percentage of people who absolutely cannot operate a pendulum is extremely low, less than 1 percent.

You can only learn to use a pendulum by practicing with it

regularly. As with any divination tool, it takes a lot of practice to become proficient and reliable with the pendulum. However, pendulum divining is the easiest and fastest of all divining methods to learn.

## STONES FOR PENDULUMS
The following list includes only those stones that are not too costly and that one may find carved into pendulum shapes. Sometimes you can find an appropriately shaped stone for a pendulum that was made to wear as a pendant.

*Agate:* balance on all levels; victory; protection against danger.

*Agate, Eye:* connection with the guardian spirit.

*Agate, Moss:* good for finding a new house, job, or relocation site.

*Amazonite:* self-confidence; creativity; communication.

*Amber:* past lives.

*Amethyst:* develop psychic abilities; increase spirituality; healing.

*Aquamarine:* banish fears; balance emotions; calmness; protection.

*Aventurine:* good health; centering; good luck.

*Beryl:* innovative thoughts; increase psychic awareness; find hidden things.

*Bloodstone:* protection from deception; good health; prosperity.

*Carnelian:* balancing; self-confidence; drives away evil.
*Chalcedony:* protection during travel; cleanses the aura.
*Chrysocolla:* protection; releases tension; enhances communication.
*Chrysoprase:* reveals the truth; balances actions and attitudes.
*Citrine:* raises self-esteem; working with karma; prosperity.
*Fluorite:* grounds energy, heals, cleanses the aura, past lives.
*Hematite:* grounds; builds courage; dissolves stress.
*Jade, Blue:* neutralizes karmic influences; relaxation.
*Jade, Green:* banishes evil; calms.
*Jasper, Brown.* grounds; stabilizes.
*Jasper, Green:* heals; balances.
*Jasper, Red:* eliminates negative energies.
*Labradorite:* connects with universal energies.
*Lapis Lazuli:* releases anxiety; increases creativity and psychic abilities.
*Malachite:* repels evil; removes subconscious blockages; heals.
*Obsidian, Black:* eliminates negatives.
*Obsidian, Snowflake:* balances; prosperity; protection.
*Onyx, Black:* deflects and destroys negative energies.
*Quartz Crystal, Clear:* protects; enhances communication with the spirit world.
*Quartz Crystal, Rose:* balances emotions; brings love; heals.
*Quartz Crystal, Smoky:* grounds and centers; breaks up subconscious blocks; strengthens the psychic.

*Tiger's Eye:* gives clear insight into problems; brings good luck; past lives.

*Tourmaline, Blue:* calms; gives clarity of insight.

*Tourmaline, Dark Green:* attracts money and success.

*Tourmaline, Red:* releases buried emotions and past sorrows.

*Tourmaline, Watermelon:* removes imbalances; solves problems.

*Turquoise:* protects; balances; enhances communication; strengthens the psychic.

# CHAPTER 3

# Divination with Pendulums

One of the most popular reasons for working with a pendulum is to use it to divine the future. Almost everyone is concerned about what the future will bring, particularly in the areas of health, love, and prosperity. What one needs to learn about this facet of pendulum divining, or any divining tool or system, is that the answers are only about possible outcomes, not a rock-solid future. The greater the number of people involved in the events surrounding an outcome, the more possibility there is for change. All it takes is one or more of the people involved to change their minds on even the smallest of decisions, and the future path of the event or question changes.

These possibilities are covered by the law of free will, something for which we should be thankful. I do not believe that our lives are predestined, with no opportunities to forge our own futures through personal decisions. There is always free will, which is a powerful force for change and diverting the life path. If you receive a divination prediction that you consider negative or not to your liking, you can change the course of your life and reactions to events, thus creating changes in the outcome itself. Granted, the outcome still may not be what you want, but it will be different than the divination predicted. Continued and numerous changes in the life path are required in order to create major changes in the outcome.

Be very careful, however, that you are not trying to control another person in any way when you set your goals or try to change a divination outcome. No one has a right to control another person or her/his future. Think how you would feel if someone did this to you against your wishes.

To prepare yourself for using the pendulum as a prediction tool, you must work long and hard to acquire the necessary skills and experience. A pendulum will react to your thoughts and instructions much faster the more you use it. Its movements will also become stronger. However, no one is infallible, so never assume that you won't ever make mistakes.

You are most apt to run into trouble predicting with a pendulum if you are asking questions for yourself or someone emotionally close to you. The more emotionally involved you allow yourself to be, the less likely you will get a truthful answer from your pendulum. The test of an experienced pendulum diviner is that she/he truly can separate her/his emotions from the questions, thus entering a neutral emotional state while working with the pendulum. This is very difficult to do.

There are a number of exercises you can do with a pendulum to increase your proficiency and the pendulum's reliability. It is best to begin with simple exercises that reinforce your communication skills with your subconscious mind. Since even predictions with a pendulum require that you ask a series of appropriate questions, the following little exercises will build your confidence and ability in selecting questions.

Fill one glass with tap water and another glass with bottled water. Set them about two hand lengths apart on a table (Figure 11, page 115). Hold the pendulum between them while asking whether the contents in both glasses are water. The pendulum should say Yes. Then ask whether the glasses both contain the same kind of water. You should get a No answer. Ask the pendulum to indicate the glass containing the tap water. It should swing directly at the appropriate glass. Finish by asking it to show you the glass of bottled water, and it will swing toward that glass. Repeat the same exercises with two glasses of tap water. Ask again if the glasses contain the same kind of water. This time the answer should be a Yes.

You have worked your way through a series of questions to discover the truth about the glasses of water. Although both glasses contain water, there are subtle differences in the composition of that water. This is the same procedure you need to adopt whenever you ask the pendulum questions. One question and its answer will not cover all the possible facets of a problem or event. By carefully wording your series of questions, you can cover all areas of an initial question and give a broader, more comprehensive answer. You may also discover that what you thought was an answer is something different when all facets of the problem are exposed.

Using a regular deck of playing cards, remove all the Jokers from the deck. Select six black cards and one red card. Shuffle these cards and lay them out face down in a line on the table (Figure 12, page 116). Do not look at the cards. The object is to discover which cards are black and which one is red. Hold the pendulum over each card as you ask whether the card is black. The pendulum should respond to one card with a No, for it will be red. Keep track of how many you get right.

When you score more correct finds than wrong ones in the last exercise, select five red cards and one black card. Shuffle these, laying them face down in a line on the table without looking at them. See if you can find the black card.

The next step is to shuffle the entire deck minus the Jokers and lay out seven cards in a line on the table. This will be more difficult, as you are not selecting a certain number of red or black cards. Keep track of your score as you hold the pendulum over one card at a time and ask about the color. Since the card will be either red or black, it does not matter which color you name when asking the question.

When you reach a high success rate at this, separate the face cards (Kings, Queens, Jacks, and Jokers) from the deck. Shuffle these cards and lay them face down on the table without looking at the cards. Now use the pendulum to search out certain cards, such as the Kings (Figure 13, page 117). Since this exercise is more involved than the previous ones, you will need to work your way through a series of questions until the pendulum gives you a Yes. For example, you may ask the pendulum if the card is a King. If it answers No, you must work your way through the list of possibilities until the pendulum gives you a Yes.

Practice the exercises with the cards until you feel confident enough to move on to the more difficult exercises that follow.

The next exercises require the help of a friend. Choose three different small objects, or coins of three different denominations. Look at the objects or coins so you will know what they are. Have a friend hide them under three opaque cups while you are not watching (Figure 14, page 118). Since you know what the objects are, ask the pendulum what is under each cup. For example, the friend has put a nickel, dime, and quarter under the cups. If you ask the pendulum if the coin under the cup is a dime, and it says No, work your way through the list of possibilities.

You may find that you have difficulty divining an object if it is hidden under a cup of a certain type of material. This may vary from pendulum to pendulum or from person to person. One dowser I know has difficulty divining anything under a particular brand of margarine container. I do not know the reason for this, but I suspect it may have to do with the material of which either the pendulum or the container is made. Perhaps the vibrations of the pendulum are such that they do not mesh well with the vibrations of the cup or container.

The next exercise is more difficult than the last one as you must now divine physical human vibrations left on an object. Have someone hold one of three coins for about twenty seconds before putting the three coins under the cups. Use the pendulum to determine which coin the person held. This practice is similar to psychometry, which is reading the vibrations of an object. However, you are doing the psychometry without seeing or touching the object in question. Practice by having different people hold a coin, then finding it. In rare occurrences, a person will be able to block her/his vibrations from reaching the coin. In this case, you will have difficulty finding the proper coin. However, it is very unlikely that this will happen.

Have someone hide one coin under a cup in a line of three cups (Figure 15, page 119) while you are not watching. Find the coin with the pendulum. You can do this by holding the pendulum over each cup as you ask the question, or by asking the pendulum to indicate which cup in the line holds the coin. This exercise is preparing you for learning map dowsing or property dowsing. If you have trouble finding the coin, hold a coin of similar denomination in one hand while using the pendulum with the other. This practice is identical to the method used by dowsers for finding missing people, water, oil, or minerals.

The following exercise is very similar to the old parlor game of Hide the Thimble; a thimble was hidden somewhere in a room and everyone tried to discover where it was by a series of questions that were answered by Hot or Cold. Have a friend choose an object in a room but not tell you what the object is. Use the pendulum to discover what the object is. For example, the friend has chosen a small statue. Begin by asking the pendulum to indicate the direction in the room in which the object lies. By a series of questions, slowly work your way through the objects in that area of the room until you discover the chosen statue. Or you can hold the pendulum over each object in that area while asking whether this is the chosen object.

Next, sketch out a floor plan of your home. Then have the

friend choose an object in your house in any of the rooms, again not revealing to you the choice of either the object or the room (Figure 16, page 120). Begin your search by holding the pendulum over the house sketch and asking which room the object is in. When you decide which room you need to search, go to that room. Ask the pendulum which area of the room contains the object you are to find. When it indicates a specific area, work your way through the objects in that area until you discover what the object is.

You have now hopefully worked your way through the preceding exercises until you are more confident of your abilities and your pendulum. If you think carefully about these exercises, you will see the important connection to divining the future or prediction methods with the pendulum. The exercises have been teaching you to explore all possible facets of a question. One question should lead to another, until you reach a definite answer. Now you are ready to take the first step into the psychic arena of future predicting.

Before asking the pendulum to answer any question of a predictive nature, or any question for that matter, you must formulate that question as clearly as possible, the shorter the better. Be very certain you do not combine two questions or ask a question that cannot be answered with a Yes or a No.

Avoid asking questions out of curiosity or those that pry

into the lives of others. These types of questions are an invasion of privacy and basically are immoral in intent. The same applies to questions whose answers might harm the interests of other people.

Each time before you ask the pendulum to answer a question, you should have it show you the Yes, No, Confusion/Wrong Question, and Neutral/Search movements. This re-establishes the code with your subconscious mind.

After doing this, and before asking a question, you need to ask the pendulum to clarify some other important points. Ask, "Am I ready to know the answer?" You might think you want an answer because your left-brain is pushing to have something resolved. The left-brain is very good at deluding us and pushing issues so they can be gotten out of the way. However, your subconscious mind and right-brain might know that you cannot handle or understand a truthful answer at this time; or that this is not the right time for the action, event, or goal you are asking about. The same applies if you are asking a question for another person. If the pendulum says No, either do not ask the question or try rephrasing the question. If the pendulum still says No, leave the question for a time before asking again.

The next question is just as important. Ask, "May I ask this question?" You have no idea sometimes if you are asking about a karmic issue that is best left alone at this time. If the pendulum says No and you ask the question anyway, you will not be able to rely on a truthful answer. If you are asking a question for another person, you have no idea whether she/he is telling the entire truthful situation behind the question.

Never answer a question about a third person for anyone. This is prying into a private area that is not any of your business or the business of the person asking. The only exception to this rule is if a mother with young children asks about them. If a spouse or lover asks about the fidelity of a partner, she/he already guesses at the answer and does not need you to confirm or deny anything. She/he must take the responsibility of making a decision on her/his own. Occasionally you may get a partner asking this question out of paranoia. In these cases it is best to avoid divining for the person at all. Nothing you say will be heard as you say it, but as she/he wants it to be.

The third question also can be vital in getting an accurate answer from your pendulum. Ask, "Do I have enough skills with divining to find the correct answer?" Sometimes a question must turn into a long series of questions, all carefully phrased, before the situation is fully explored. This question is vitally important if you plan to attempt to find an object or missing person. Finding an object in a house with a pendulum is an entirely different set of circumstances than trying to find an object lost elsewhere or a missing, and possibly deceased, person. Every time a person is missing, the police are flooded with calls from would-be psychics who think they know where the person is, and who would love the publicity if the person were found. However, accurate, useful information of this kind is extremely rare. Using a pendulum to search in this manner requires a lot of practice and experience. Even then, most people do not have the intuitive connection to accurately find anyone.

Getting correct answers from a pendulum is not by chance, but a matter of practice and experience. Now that you are aware of all the necessary steps to future divining, you are ready to ask your pendulum a question pertaining to your own future. Always practice on yourself before you jump into trying to answer questions for others.

Think very carefully about a question you want answered about your future. Word the question so that it can be answered with a Yes or a No. Shuffle a tarot deck and choose nine cards at random. If you do not have tarot cards, you can use rune cards or rune stones. Hold the pendulum over each card and ask if that particular card is important to the question you have in mind (Figure 17, page 121). If you are not familiar with the meanings of the tarot cards or runes, look up each card in its accompanying book and see how it pertains to your question. Think about the pendulum answers, for the cards may point out new options or challenges that you had not considered.

Do not think about the answer you want or any answer at all, for that matter. Doing this will interfere with a truthful reply from the pendulum. Instead, think, "I wonder what the answer will be." Since the left-brain always requires something to occupy its attention and keep it from interfering with the answer from the right-brain, thinking of such a statement will occupy your left-brain's time and let the real answer slip through unimpeded.

Perhaps you have so many questions about your future you cannot decide where to begin. Figure 18 (page 122) is a fan chart that can help you choose the most important aspect of your life to inquire about with your pendulum. Often the area we think is the most important to a positive future is not, under the surface, the correct one at all. If you are elsewhere when asking this question and do not have access to this book, you can draw out a circle on a piece of paper and divide it into four quarters. Label the quarters as physical, mental, social, and spiritual. Circle dowsing is more difficult, however, unless you have years of practice.

Most pendulum charts are designed on either the circle or the fan layout. The circle layout is self-explanatory: a circle with marked segments that meet in the center. When using this layout, hold the pendulum over the center of the chart. However, dowsing on a circle chart can be confusing as to which segment the pendulum is indicating. For this reason I have chosen to use only fan charts in this book.

The fan chart is shaped like an Oriental fan with one flat edge at the bottom. The marked segments all converge in the center of the flat edge. To work with this layout, hold the pendulum over the center of the bottom edge where all the lines converge when you ask a question.

Now, ask the pendulum to indicate the area of your future that is most important to you at this time and to the goals you wish to accomplish. Or, you can ask which area you should be most concerned with. When your pendulum has answered, think seriously about the area indicated, for you may have missed the possibility of future trouble in that part of your life. This will make you more aware of problems before they get out of hand. It also will help you to eliminate problems by making changes.

Sometimes the areas of Figure 18 are not specific enough for your needs. Figure 19 (page 123) is a fan chart that is divided to better clarify life areas. It is divided into seven parts or segments, labeled: career, finances, love, health, mental, family, and spiritual. Hold the pendulum over the point where all the lines come together at the bottom. Ask the question, "Which part of my life needs work?" Again, seriously consider the answer the pendulum gives you. In creating the best future for yourself, you cannot afford to overlook even the smallest hints.

If you dread getting an answer about one area of your life, your emotions will interfere with an accurate pendulum reading. Separation of personal emotions from your pendulum work is the only way to reach the truth. The area you most dread to hear about may be the very one the pendulum will help you in solving. Remember not to think of the answer you want or even of an answer you dread. Keep as much of a neutral emotional state as possible by concentrating on "I wonder what the answer will be."

You now have all of the basics of pendulum divining that are necessary to divine the future for yourself or anyone else. Please use these methods with integrity, ethics, and morals, keeping your ego and sense of self-importance out of it.

Figure 20 (page 124) is a fan chart for Yes/No/Maybe Yes/Maybe No. I did not mention this chart before as I feel it is important for a pendulum user to learn the basics without relying on a chart. I have included this particular chart to help those beginners who may feel they do not have what it takes to work with a pendulum. Such people can start with this chart as an aid, but I encourage all dowsers to become self-sufficient and dispense with the use of this particular chart as soon as possible.

To work the Yes/No/Maybe chart, hold the pendulum over the center of the flat edge where all the lines converge. Dowsers call this point the hinge. Make certain your question is formulated to have only one answer. The pendulum then will move toward the marked segment that it sees as correct.

Sometimes the pendulum will swing on a line between two segments. If this happens, you must decide if the question has been formulated properly. If the answer is questionable, or if you wish further confirmation, ask the pendulum whether this question can be answered at all. If it answers Yes, reformulate your question and try again. If you still get an idiot answer, do not ask again for a period of time. Remember, do not think of the answer you want.

Pendulum divining or dowsing can be very helpful in choosing the right path in your life, whether the issue at stake is small or large. However, you should never become so dependent on any divination tool that you fear to make a move without consulting it. Use your pendulum responsibly. It is not a toy, nor is it the supreme answer to every single problem. However, the pendulum can be a wonderful tool for opening your subconscious mind and letting the needed, correct answers surface.

CHAPTER 4

# Balancing and Healing with Pendulums

$F$ew dowsers or diviners are good at all uses of the pendulum. Some are very good at dowsing in health matters, but cannot find water underground. Some are excellent in witching for water or oil, but have no luck whatsoever in using a pendulum to answer other questions. You should try all methods of using the pendulum before you decide that some applications of dowsing will or will not work for you. It is also probable that with practice, patience, and experience you can learn to use the pendulum in any area of dowsing you wish to explore.

Personal health and the health of your family are of prime importance to all people. With the cost of insurance and medical care skyrocketing, each person must be as well informed as possible. Giving your doctor polite suggestions to help with diagnoses and knowing something about an illness can cut medical costs and give you a greater chance for a quick recovery.

This makes learning how to heal and balance the four main bodies of humans well worth the effort.

Although a pendulum can be very useful in diagnosing illnesses, you should never make medical recommendations for others. This can get you into serious trouble with the police and the American Medical Association. Also, you should never diagnose for another person unless she/he specifically asks you to do so.

In asking about health matters, perhaps more than with any other questions, the dowser must take great care to detach the emotions from the question. You have to work at not thinking about an answer while waiting for the pendulum to move. Keep telling yourself, "I wonder what it will be?" or keep repeating the question to block out expectant thoughts. Otherwise, your pendulum will give you the answer you want, not necessarily the truthful one.

The best place to begin learning the healing techniques with a pendulum is to learn how to diagnose and balance your own seven main chakras of your astral body. The chakras are part of the Hindu tradition, and are frequently called "light centers" or "wheels of light." The chakras are called "wheels" because they appear to spin. The seven chakras can be diagnosed with a pendulum for imbalance in much the same manner as the physical body can be. All diseases of the physical will appear first in the astral body, via the chakras and the aura.

Although there are more than seven chakras in the astral body, I will talk about only the seven most commonly known ones. The first (red) lies at the base of the spine, the second (orange) midway between the navel and pelvic region, the third (yellow) near the navel, the fourth (green) at the center of the chest, the fifth (blue) at the base of the throat, the sixth (purple) between the eyebrows, and the seventh (lavender or white) at the top of the head. There are also powerful chakras in the palm of each hand and the sole of each foot, plus a number of lesser chakras in various places over the body. Although I will not discuss these last-mentioned chakras, it is important that you know they exist. Figure 21a (page 125) is a fan chart for dowsing the chakras. See Figure 21b (page 126) for traditional chakra placement of the seven main chakras.

Chakras can become blocked, over- or under-stimulated, or out of balance because of approaching diseases, negative emotions, or stressful events. You can use your pendulum to recharge and rebalance them.

Since holding your pendulum over each of your own chakras, as you would with another person, would be difficult, there is another technique you can use. Purchase film sheets of the appropriate chakra colors from a photographic store.

These film sheets are commonly used over a camera lens to change the color. If you cannot find film sheets, you can use squares of colored paper. From these sheets, cut a 1–1 1/2 inch square of each color. Put these squares in the correct order, beginning with red for the first chakra and ending with lavender for the seventh one.

The chakras in the palms of the hands are associated with giving and receiving, so you will use them to properly input energy to any imbalanced chakra. By using the pendulum and the colored squares in the palm of your hand, you can avoid overcharging these "light" centers.

Begin by placing the red square in the palm of one hand. Hold the pendulum over this colored square with your other hand. If any of your chakras do not need balancing, the pendulum will not move or will move very little. If the chakra does need balancing, the pendulum will circle clockwise until the adjustment has been made. Then it will stop. When the pendulum stops, lay aside the red square and place the next color (orange) in your palm. Repeat with the pendulum over it. Keep changing colored squares and checking with the pendulum until you have gone through all the colors, ending with lavender.

If working on another person, have her/him lie on the back while you hold the pendulum over each chakra area. You can have the person lie on her/his stomach if you wish, but most healers seem to work more efficiently on the front of the body instead of on the back. Hindu tradition says that the chakras radiate outward from the spine toward the front of the body. Hold the pendulum over each chakra, beginning at the base of the spine and ending at the top of the head. The pendulum will indicate a Yes or forward and backward motion if the chakra is balanced, a No or side-to-side movement if it is out of balance. Occasionally, a balanced, unblocked chakra will cause the pendulum to move in a clockwise direction, while imbalance will make the pendulum move counterclockwise.

When you discover an out-of-balance chakra, place the appropriate colored square on that chakra. The pendulum will swing in a clockwise direction until the adjustment is complete.

If you prefer to work on a more impersonal level when divining the chakras, or the person requesting the healing is absent, use the chakra chart and a photo of the person involved. Touch the position of each chakra on the chakra chart or photo while asking the pendulum to show you if it is balanced. If the pendulum indicates No, place the appropriate colored square on the chart or photo. Hold the pendulum over the square until its clockwise movement has finished.

Although there are more chakras than the seven listed, the imbalance or blockage of these seven is more apt to cause physical disease or distress. To diagnose with the pendulum for disease, instead of searching for imbalanced chakras, you need to know what imbalance in each chakra can mean in the way of diseases. The following suggestions will differ somewhat from other chakra discussions, for each healer will approach chakra healing a little differently.

In this case, the first chakra represents the spine, bones, rectum, legs, intestinal tract, the circulatory system, and the blood itself. The second chakra is for the reproductive system and sex organs, the kidneys, urinary tract, and digestion. The third chakra symbolizes the liver, gallbladder, pancreas, and the entire nervous system. The fourth chakra represents the heart, the skin, the lower portion of the lungs, and the hands. The fifth chakra is for the throat, the top portion of the lungs and the bronchia, the thyroid gland, and the voice. The sixth chakra regulates the face along with the ears, eyes, and nose; it also affects the cerebellum portion of the brain. The seventh chakra represents the skull and the rest of the brain. Some healers also list the seventh chakra as an indicator of the health of the soul.

For example, you find that the pendulum indicates that the second chakra of the person you are testing has something wrong. The pendulum is swinging in a counterclockwise or side-to-side direction, indicating a No. You ask if the problem is in the reproductive system. The pendulum says No. You proceed down the list of possible diseases, asking about the sex organs, the kidneys, and digestion, receiving a No each time. When you ask about the urinary tract, the pendulum says Yes.

You now place the orange square over the approximate area of the second chakra, then hold the pendulum about 6 inches above the square. The pendulum will swing in a clockwise direction until it has fed in as much chakra energy as it can. Although this procedure will help the patient with the disease, you should instruct the person to see her/his physician as soon as possible for a checkup. Do not diagnose or prescribe treatments. A urinary tract problem can range from an infection to kidney stones.

Frequently, a health problem associated with a chakra is more difficult to pinpoint, or does not seem to be entirely related to a specific chakra. The pendulum user then must go beyond diagnosis through the chakras, and use the pendulum over the entire body in a slightly different manner. In this case, the pendulum will respond with a clockwise or forward and backward motion (a Yes) for good health and a counterclockwise or side-to-side motion (a No) for ill health, damage, or disease.

When determining what part of a human body is in need of

treatment, have the patient lie on her/his back while you slowly move the pendulum about 6 inches above the body. Begin at the head and work down to the feet. Remember to take your time, as the pendulum must be given an opportunity to respond. Cover the entire front of the body, then have the patient lie on her/his stomach and repeat the procedure with the pendulum.

The pendulum will give a Yes or positive movement over areas in good health. It will give a No or negative movement over areas in which there is disease, imbalance, or pending health problems.

If the person to be diagnosed cannot be present, you can work with a full photo of the person by using a pointer to touch each area while holding the pendulum in the other hand. After you have gained much experience in this form of pendulum diagnosis, you can work on a person even if no photo is available. You do this by holding the person in mind while you use the pendulum over pictures in an anatomy book. However, it is much easier to work from a photo.

This method of pendulum dowsing will reveal not only present problems, but also past injuries and even surgeries. It will be common for irregularities to appear in the neck and shoulders where stress and tension accumulate. Past injuries also will show up in this examination, particularly to the back and joints. Before you state that the patient has problems in any area indicated by the pendulum, be certain to ask her/him if there was a past disease, injury, or surgery in that area.

A simple exercise will show you that the pendulum does indeed pick up injuries, however slight. Sit in a chair and hold your pendulum over one of your thighs. Ask about the health of your thigh, and observe what motion the pendulum makes over that particular leg. Then slap your other hand sharply against the same thigh. Observe what the pendulum now does. You will get two entirely different readings from your pendulum.

A pendulum will not only tell you what part of the body is ill, it also can help you determine the cause behind the bodily sickness. The whole person consists of four bodies: physical, mental, emotional, and spiritual. An imbalance in any one of these bodies will affect the other three, and open the immune system to the possibility of disease. It is very rare that all four of these bodies are in perfect alignment at any one time. It is considered to be average if two out of the four bodies are in balance (Figure 22, page 127).

The chart for physical cause of a disease (Figure 23, page 128) will help the diviner in pinpointing any specific physical source that is detrimental to the inquirer. If nothing is pertinent on this chart, or you suspect that there may be more than one cause, try the chart for psychic cause of a disease (Figure 24, page 129). This chart deals with emotional and mental causes. However, the segment "psychic attack" should not be taken to mean "black magic" or "spellworking." It is more likely that the psychic attack will be a build-up of jealousy, hatred, or a deep desire for control or punishment that comes from another person or persons, rather than a deliberate effort to use magic against someone. This same build-up within a person often can be the cause of disease inflicted upon herself/himself.

Animals can also be diagnosed in the same way with a pendulum to see if they are ill and may need a veterinary. Pets are dependent upon their owners to be observant and get them health care when they need it. Although many pets develop a psychic or telepathic bond with the owner, they cannot always tell us exactly what the problem is, no more than we often can tell our physician the exactness of a disease. The only problem you may have in dowsing a pet for health is that it might consider the swinging pendulum a fascinating toy.

There is also much discussion on whether animals have the same number of chakras as humans, and whether these chakras are in the same positions. I believe animals do have the same number of chakras and surrounding astral bodies as humans do. Those who do not believe this base their theories on the idea that animals are less evolved. Having observed animals and humans for many years, I cannot subscribe to these theories. I have seen animals that have more common sense, compassion, and spirituality than quite a few humans.

Another interesting and useful area of pendulum dowsing is that of finding and reading the human aura. Although there actually is more than one human aura surrounding us, it is best to skip this esoteric information and concentrate on the one main body aura. Before trying to read the aura, you should learn to use your pendulum simply to find the aura on another person and determine how far out it extends from the physical body.

Have the test person sit in a chair while you slowly move the pendulum around her/his body. For beginners, it is easiest to find the aura around the head and shoulders. Begin by holding the pendulum about 4 to 6 inches away from the top of the head. Ask the pendulum to show you where the person's aura is. It will respond with a Yes movement if it is within the aura field. Move the pendulum out an inch or so more, and ask the same question again. Repeat this until you have reached the outer limits of the aura, when the pendulum will answer with a No motion. You also can do this with plants, animals, and inanimate objects, such as rocks (Figure 25, page 130).

You may find that certain areas of a person's aura may be closer to the body or much farther out than the average range of the aura. This is an indication of a disease or potential illness. When you discover such a depression or flare, you then must use your pendulum to determine if the problem is physical, mental, emotional, or spiritual. You do this by asking whether the problem is of a physical nature. If the pendulum answers with a No, work your way through the other three categories. Sometimes, the pendulum will indicate that none of these areas are responsible for the depression or flare. If this happens, you need to ask whether the reason is a karmic one. If the answer is a Yes, read chapter 6, "Dowsing in the Field of Past Lives, Karma, and Reincarnation."

Pendulum dowsing can also be used to help in personal health and diet. However, you should only use this aspect of dowsing on yourself and your immediate family. Do not make recommendations or take action to eliminate or add something to your diet and lifestyle without exploring more deeply the fields of herbalism and vitamins.

Using a pendulum, you can test whether certain vitamins and foods are good for you and which will cause problems. A good example is to set out a cup of tea or coffee. See what the pendulum says about your reaction to the drink. Then ask whether you should add any cream or sugar. Use the pendulum over another beverage, such as a soda. Is it good for you? Before deciding to take action one way or another, carefully think about how you feel when you ingest these beverages. Did you experience digestion problems, or a nervous reaction? If you answer Yes, consider eliminating the beverage in question for a few days and see what happens. The beverage itself may not be to blame. It may cause negative reactions only when combined with certain other foods.

If you suspect that a new food may give you digestive problems, use your pendulum to find out for certain. Then sample the food in question in very small quantities to see what the reaction will be.

You can also use the pendulum to test your physical reactions to food additives, sweets, or foods you ordinarily eat. Some of us eat certain foods all our lives and wonder why we suffer digestive problems. Often, it is not the food itself, but whatever is added to it or on it. In determining the negative or positive reaction of your body to a food, phrase your questions carefully, and be certain that you cover all possibilities, from additives and sprays to how the food is cooked and in what.

If you suffer an unpleasant reaction such as bloating after an ordinary meal, use your pendulum to discover which food caused the problem. It may even be a combination of foods. Since the body changes over time, what you could eat without distress at one time may not be good for you at a later date or as you age. For example, you may eat raw onions with impunity until you reach middle age. Then you might find that you only can tolerate cooked onions in small amounts.

The pendulum can be a valuable tool in discovering which vitamins you may need or should eliminate from your daily health routine. The same divining process can be used to test herbs.

While you are using the pendulum to test food, vitamins, or herbs, you should avoid thinking about any specific theory or health report. This can result in an incorrect answer. If the mind wanders while dowsing, it overrides the link you must create with all your senses and awareness. It divides your focus and breaks the contact with the subconscious mind.

Hold the vitamin or herb in one hand while holding your pendulum in the other. Ask if the vitamin or herb is helpful to you. If the pendulum answers with a firm No, you should reconsider keeping the vitamin or herb as part of your daily regime. If the answer is a Confusion movement, you need to question further if the substance reacts negatively when combined with other vitamins or herbs, or whether it is a supplement that you should not use on a daily basis, but is fine to use once a week or so.

Even if the pendulum gives you a firm Yes answer, you need to go a step further and ask if the substance is one you can take every day, or whether you should skip days. Never rely on a single answer. You must explore the full parameters of the product. Also, what your body needs during one phase of your life may not be appropriate at another time.

# CHAPTER 5

# Map and Ground Dowsing

$A$ pendulum is a very versatile tool, good for purposes beyond divination and healing. It also can be used to trace underground water lines, storage tanks, earth energy lines, power spots, or ancient sites. Dowsing for underground pipes or tanks is nothing new. Although not highly publicized, this technique was taught to soldiers in the Vietnam war to help them find underground bunkers. Since the soldiers did not have pendulums, they were taught to make L-rods out of bent coat hangers.

Dowsing for earth energy, water, oil, or minerals is a process of listening to your intuition. Intuition cannot be proved in a lab or in a test atmosphere because "knowing" something intuitively is not provable. The dowser seems to pick up signals from the earth subconsciously, such as moving streams of water, a certain feeling for oil and coal, or a subconscious reaction to certain minerals. One theory that makes the most sense is that all humans are part of the universe and can be sensitive to whatever else is part of the universe. When you open your subconscious mind and listen to your intuition, you are using a kind of radar to search for the vibrations of something you want to find.

Dowsing or divining is usually connected by the human mind with finding water or oil. These are very specialized fields and require a lot of practice and the asking of very specific questions. Dowsing is often called witching, as in a water witch who looks for water. A water witch who is really good at dowsing will be accurate between 85 and 90 percent of the time. Although most water, oil, and mineral dowsing is done with L-rods or forked sticks, there is no reason one cannot use a pendulum. Since a pendulum is more affected by body motion than L-rods or forked sticks, however, the dowser will have to walk very slowly, frequently coming to a full stop to see how the pendulum reacts.

The best way to learn dowsing for water is to dowse for underground water lines. Pendulum reaction to moving water in lines can be in two ways. The pendulum may respond with a Yes or positive movement when you slowly walk over the pipe's position. Or, it may swing in the direction in which the pipe lies (Figure 26, page 131). When you stand directly above the pipe, the pendulum may go into the Search or Neutral movement, or may circle wildly in a clockwise motion.

Beginners in dowsing need to be aware that it is only running or flowing underground water that makes the pendulum react. This action can be affected by water or sewer lines that have running water in them at the time of the dowsing. This is helpful if you are seeking the whereabouts of water or sewer lines, but not if you are seeking a new source of water. If you dowse a piece of land for water, be sure that you mark out any known sources of water before you begin.

Many dowsers who use the pendulum to locate underground pipes use what is known as the Bishop's Rule. This rule will aid you in determining how deep in the ground the pipe lies. First, find the pipe and mark its location. Then ignore the pipe and ask the pendulum to show you its depth. Slowly walk outward from the pipe's location until the pendulum responds with a Yes or positive movement. You must move slowly, as the pipe can be anywhere from a few inches to a few feet down. The distance from the pipe should match its depth. The same principle applies to new and untapped underground sources of water.

Because each dowser is different, the pendulum may respond by giving you the depth in a different manner. Some dowsers find that their device will measure the distance of the depth at half or twice the length walked. Experience is the only way to judge which works for you. Personally, I have little luck in determining depth.

Dowsing for other substances, such as oil or minerals, is much the same as dowsing for water. The pendulum will react with a firm, sometimes very rapid, clockwise circling when the dowser walks over an area that contains the sought substance. To aid in the search, some dowsers use the metal pendulum that has a twist-off top and interior cavity. They will put a small amount of the sought substance into the pendulum cavity, thus working on the theory that like substances attract. Others merely will hold a tiny glass vial of the substance in their other hand.

There also is another method that can be used for finding a substance. You may ask the pendulum, "Show me the direction in which _____ is." This question can save you time, as the pendulum's method of movement will help you determine whether you are moving in the correct direction. You must watch the outer edge of the pendulum swing for clues. This outer edge of the swing is called the leading edge by dowsers (Figure 27, page 132). If the pendulum swings forward and backward, you are facing in the right direction to search for the object. If it swings clockwise or counterclockwise, turn in the direction of the swing and try again. Any time you are directly facing the object sought, the pendulum will swing forward and backward. A clockwise or counterclockwise swing will turn you full circle in about fifteen tries.

You can use triangulation to further pinpoint an object. When you have a forward and backward swing of the pendulum, move to another spot and repeat the question. Do this until you get another forward and backward swing of the pendulum. Then mentally draw a line from where you stood in both places. Where the lines intersect, you will find the object you seek. (Figure 28, page 133).

Trying to find an object or substance on a sketched map of a house or property with a pendulum is more difficult and requires that you ask a series of appropriate questions. The questions must be phrased for Yes or No answers, as in "Am I facing the right direction to find _____?" This question requires that you move only slightly to face a new direction.

Another method, if you know the general area in which you lost something, is to do a triangulation first. Then walk slowly in the direction indicated, holding the pendulum before you. The pendulum will swing in an oval path, with the leading edge pointing in the correct direction. When you are directly over the object, the pendulum swing will change to a circle motion. If you pass beyond the object, the pendulum will once more swing in an oval. Some people use this method to find studs in interior walls or the part of a machine that is not working properly.

If something is lost within your house, draw a floor plan of all the rooms (Figure 29, page 134). Then use the pendulum over each room until you find the room containing the lost object. As with map dowsing, you can point to a room or area of a room with one finger or a pencil while asking the pendulum questions. Then go to the chosen room and ask the pendulum to show you the direction in which the object lies. Remember to move only a little at a time as you work your way around a room.

Map dowsing requires much the same technique as finding an object within a house. Map dowsing can be used to find underground water, minerals, or missing persons. It also can be used to find the general location of an appropriate house or apartment, if you are searching for somewhere to move. To begin, you need a regular map of an area. Using your finger or a pencil, slowly point to various areas on the map until you get a positive response from the pendulum. You may find that the pendulum responds to more than one area. After you have discovered a general area in which you may find what you are seeking, you need a larger scale map that has more details. Again, slowly point out various spots in the larger scale map until the pendulum swings in a positive or Yes motion (Figure

30, page 135). You can work the information down to a specific block or street. However, it is easier to go to the area and look for yourself at this point. For example, if you are seeking a house, have a real estate agent run a check for available houses in that area.

An experienced map dowser can find anything she/he sets the mind on. Ordinary maps are useful only for wide area dowsing. To find anything in a very specific place, you will need the largest scale map you can get. Begin by asking the pendulum if what you seek is on the map at all. Sometimes what the conscious mind perceives as the correct area for the object sought is totally incorrect. A map featuring every road, city block, or other details is needed to pinpoint exact locations. Hold the pendulum over the map with your dowsing hand while slowly pointing to one small area after another with a pointer or pen in your other hand. Each time you move the pen, ask the pendulum again if this area contains what you seek. When you touch the correct area, the pendulum will respond with a Yes.

Many people are familiar with the dowsing done along the ley-lines in England, but are unaware that these energy lines exist everywhere, encircling the entire earth. It is quite common for underground streams of water to flow along or very close to these lines. When a vein of water reaches the surface along one of these energy lines, it is sometimes called a holy well. Dowsers call this water "juvenile water," meaning that it does not go through the evaporation and rain cycle, but bubbles up from deep within the earth and frequently has a high mineral content.

You can dowse for energy lines by walking slowly over an area and watching the pendulum movement (Figure 31, page 136). Just keep asking the pendulum to show you where the energy lines are. Until you gain experience with energy line dowsing, you should stay away from areas with underground water or sewer pipes. These can cause you to misread the pendulum movements. When you are directly over an earth energy line, the pendulum will move in a perfect circle.

If you discover a sacred place (power spot) where two or more lines meet, the pendulum will circle so fast that it will be nearly parallel to the earth. The stronger the energies in such a place, the faster the pendulum will circle. Sometimes a power spot or sacred place will appear where there are no energy lines to cross. The energy of these spots seems to reach the earth's surface directly from some central reservoir of power.

Some dowsers can discover the timing of events by pointing to calendar dates and even the numbers on a clock face. However, this type of pendulum dowsing is very untrustworthy, and you easily can be misled by your thoughts or the thoughts of another person.

To dowse for a specific ingredient, such as minerals, water, or certain stones, hold a small sample of the material in one hand while you dowse for a Yes or No answer with the other hand. To practice for this, have someone prepare three glasses of water: one plain, one with a little sugar, and one with a little salt (Figure 32, page 137). You may find that you have to increase or decrease the length of the string in order to find certain substances.

If you are interested in weather forecasting, dowsing can be a fun way to pit your skills against those of the National Weather Bureau. The National Weather Bureau's accurate prediction rate is actually quite low, about thirty percent. Get a list of the forecasts for a number of cities around the country or even around the world. Then write out a list of the cities you want to cover. You can dowse for such things as sun, rain, clouds, or temperatures. Later, you can check your accuracy.

# CHAPTER 6

# Dowsing in the Field of Past Lives, Karma, and Reincarnation

$M$ost major events and relationships in life have a karmic background. Karma is not all negative, or having to pay for past mistakes, whether in this life or other lives. Karma can also be the reaping of just and positive rewards. Sometimes we return to a relationship believing that we can help other people pay back karma or make positive changes in their lives. Too often we find ourselves in a repetitive situation in which the other person has no intention of paying back or changing. If that person's behavior and intent make it clear that she/he has no plans to repay to you the debts owed, you must face reality and take steps to remove yourself from the negative relationship.

Using your pendulum to dowse in the field of karma and reincarnation will aid you in pinpointing the cause of problems, whether with yourself and your past lives, or with others and their past lives. None of us are blameless when we find ourselves in a negative situation, based in either this life or a past one. We all contribute something to every such situation, whether this contribution is deliberate or passive. We can turn these events into positive energy only when we take responsibility to look truthfully at things and do something to better ourselves.

Often we need most to look at our own past lives and worry less about others' influence on us. Every life is composed of what went before, just as what occurred in childhood may be the basis for the way we act later. Frequently, these past lives influence us subconsciously as to the manner in which we react to certain people or experiences, the importance or unimportance that we assign to ourselves, and many of our personality quirks.

You can use your pendulum to open doors to past lives if you are careful in how you word your questions and keep your desires and emotions out of it. Never dowse for past lives with a particular destination in mind. This mental frame of mind will be certain to give you false answers. Also, do not fall into the trap of thinking you were someone famous or important in past lives. The vast majority of people were those who subtly influenced history by their common, everyday lives and decisions, not the people recorded by history as famous.

The chart of past life dates (Figures 33a–33b, pages 138–139) will help you to determine where the present influences are coming from in your past, if you ask, "What time period is the biggest influence on my present life?" These dates are divided into two charts to make it easier for the inquirer to use. Alternatively, you may use the charts to answer such questions as "When did I live my last life?" or "When did I live a past life with (name)?"

The next charts are for locating where in the time period you lived a past life. There are two charts for location to make it easier for the inquirer to use (Figures 34a–34b, pages 140–141). Frequently, the past life location indicated by the pendulum will explain why you have a deep interest in certain cultures or areas of the world.

The past life gender graph is located on the corner of the chart for the past life social background chart (Figure 35, page 142). The gender graph will help you in determining if you were male or female. Gender often changes as we go from one life to another, so that we can experience the different social restrictions and benefits of a particular time period and culture.

The past life social background chart will aid you in discovering what role you played in society and what experiences you were likely to have had. Were you in a social position that did not allow you to become all you could have been? Did you resent the unbreakable social barriers? Do you still harbor those resentments today? These questions and more must be asked if you want to know a past life in depth.

The past life occupation charts (Figures 36a–36b, pages 143–144) help to uncover the method by which you made your way in a given past life. What we once learned as a farmer may influence our present interest in gardening, or what we learned as a merchant may influence how ethically or unethically we do business today. If you wish to delve further into the occupation of a past life, you must formulate a series of carefully worded questions that will reveal what you learned from that lifetime. For example, if your pendulum indicates that you were of a religious order, you might ask:

"Did I like what I did?"
"Did I learn compassion for others?"
"Was I influenced by corruption within the religious order?"
"Did I join the order because I was forced to do so?"
"Did I rebel against the rules of the order?"

To learn the truth, you must not be afraid to cover all aspects of that life, both positive and negative.

Frequently, people who are interested in karma and past lives want to know what their relationship with family or a specific person was in that life. The chart of karmic relationship (Figure 37, page 145) will aid in getting such an answer.

Often this answer helps a person understand why there are difficulties or unpleasantness in dealing with certain people in her/his life. Just because the pendulum indicates that a specific person was a spouse in a prior life does not mean she/he is the perfect spouse this time. The person may have been cruel, unfaithful, or had addictions, some or all of which may surface in this life. Also, a perfect and loving relationship in one life may not be so perfect and loving this time. People change; that is the nature and meaning of karma. That is why I do not believe that "soul mates" are particularly associated with past relationships. What worked in a relationship long ago may well not work at all now.

A "soul mate" is a person who is the perfect complement to you in any given lifetime. Sometimes she/he does appear out of a past relationship, but more often she/he has changed and evolved into that perfect niche through lifetimes of casual acquaintance and life trials. It also is possible for there to be more than one "soul mate" available in a lifetime.

Sometimes we are blinded by the intuitive recognition of a past love with a person and do not see the unsatisfactory changes for a time—changes that have made the love no longer viable or acceptable. This frequently occurs when two people experience an immediate, strong, physical attraction, or love at first sight.

Any time you delve into the arena of past lives, you must be extremely careful to keep your emotions, desires, and prior thoughts on the matter out of your mind while dowsing with the pendulum. Your thoughts on this subject are even more apt to influence the pendulum than in the area of health and healing. However, learning about your past lives and their influence on this life can be very liberating and insightful if you take the matter seriously. Knowing where certain habits or urges originated can help you to create positive changes in yourself. Discovering the background to an uncomfortable or negative familial or sexual relationship can give you the courage to break away and build your life anew. The entire purpose of delving into past lives should be to make positive personal changes and revive past talents.

CHAPTER 7

# Obstacles, Destiny, Astrology, and Other Subjects

Now that you have learned a great many things about yourself and your pendulum, it is time to tackle the much more complex areas of pendulum dowsing. These areas definitely require that you keep a separation of your emotions and desires from your mind while dowsing or the results will be untrustworthy.

The accuracy chart (Figure 38, page 146) is self-explanatory. It is very important to use this chart each time before you begin dowsing on past lives, astrology, or the planets, as you must be assured that the pendulum's accuracy is high enough to give you the true and potentially valuable answer you seek. This chart will give you the accuracy rating of a particular pendulum at any given time. Since your emotional state and physical vitality will change from day to day or from one part of a day to another, you may wish to check the accuracy of your pendulum at that time. Any time the accuracy rate falls below 60 percent, it is best to not use that particular pendulum at that time, or not do any pendulum divining at that time.

The inaccuracy chart (Figure 39, page 147) will help you pinpoint why the pendulum is not working at peak efficiency. If you dowse on the accuracy chart and get a low figure, this chart can help you pinpoint the reason. All of the segment names are easily understood, except perhaps for the "Other People" category. People who are skeptical or who really do not want you to reveal an answer to their question can influence the pendulum's accuracy. It is also possible that your own subconscious mind is afraid to reveal the answer you say you are seeking. This negative influence also extends to people who are jealous of your abilities and wish you to fail. Remember that some pendulums simply are not useful for dowsing on certain types of questions. If a certain pendulum consistently rates a low percentage of accuracy in preparation for asking particular questions, you will need to use another pendulum.

You will notice that on one corner of some of the charts (particularly those charts that are continued in another chart) is a simple Yes/No indicator. To save time, hold your pendulum over this Yes/No and ask, "Is this the chart I need?" If the pendulum answers No, go to the next chart.

The first chart of obstacles (Figure 40, page 148) is used to reveal possible trouble ahead in events and situations. When using this chart, you should ask, "What are the obstacles ahead in this situation (name the situation)?" This chart is useful in uncovering what internal, subconscious attributes should be changed or modified to bring success.

The second chart of obstacles (Figure 41, page 149) should be used for relationship questions, such as, "What obstacles are ahead in the relationship with (name)?" Some relationships, either as friends or lovers, can create unwanted emotions if the parties involved do not look at all the little signals in complete honesty. The outcome can be totally different from what was expected.

The destiny chart (Figure 42, page 150) can be used in conjunction with either or both of the obstacles charts. It can be applied to personal or business affairs to give the inquirer clues to the outcome of an event or relationship if all things remain on the present path. Any answer indicated by the pendulum on this chart will be much more difficult to change, as it will require major changes in all aspects of your life and/or goals.

The chart for blockages (Figure 43, page 151) can help you understand what is impeding your progress toward a goal. If the pendulum indicates a particular blockage, be certain to ask more specific questions to give you a wider view of the trouble.

In using the charts of astrological houses (Figures 44a–44b, pages 152–153), you need to ask questions that have their basis in everyday life, such as family, business, social, or personal problems or goals. These two charts, which together make up the traditional astrological wheel, are even more specific than the charts of obstacles, blockages, or destiny. If you use these charts, you must be prepared to think long and hard about the indicated segment in order to determine the reason for it being chosen by the pendulum. The more personal the house and characteristics indicated, the more closely you must be willing to look. As humans, we tend to gloss over personal indications, preferring to believe that others are the source of our troubles, not ourselves.

*First House:* this house rules the physical self and the personality; in other words, the way the world sees you. It also describes influences and molding of early childhood; mannerisms; disposition and temperament; likes and dislikes; what you want in life and how you achieve it.

*Second House:* this house has to do with money; movable possessions; earning abilities and the way you handle money; self-esteem.

*Third House:* this house refers to your siblings and relatives, and the family ties you do or do not have. It also influences your knowledge; environment; short trips; communications; the way you think, speak, and write; logic; memory; manual skill; early education and the ability to learn.

*Fourth House:* this is the house of the home and immediate family; the foundation of your present life. It also points to the father's character and influence; your background and roots; what you keep protected and secluded from the world.

*Fifth House:* this area symbolizes the heart, romance, love affairs, and your sexual nature in general. It also points to children; entertainment; creativity; new undertakings; gambling; pets and playmates.

*Sixth House:* this house is for personal responsibilities, and the way you do or do not handle them. It also shows the influences of colleagues and employees; work; service to others; health; illnesses brought on by worry or emotional upsets.

*Seventh House:* an area of primary relationships and partnerships, this house reveals marriage; divorce; remarriage; business and legal affairs; contracts; open enemies; adversaries in the business world; the public.

*Eighth House:* this house points to joint resources; investments; taxes; inheritances; debts of partner; death and rebirth or regeneration; spiritual transformation; surgeries; psychic powers or knowledge; occult studies.

*Ninth House:* this is the house of social areas; higher education; philosophy; religion; law; long-distance travel; foreign places and peoples; your public expression of ideas; publishing.

*Tenth House:* this is the area of reputation; career; social responsibilities; ambition; attainment; outward expression of talents. It also reveals the mother's influence and character on your life.

*Eleventh House:* this house governs your goals; friends; social values; teamwork; long-term dreams and wishes; involvement with groups and organizations; idealism and visions.

*Twelfth House:* this last astrological house is concerned with the subconscious; past karma; privacy; retreat or confinement; prisons; hospitals; secret enemies; self-defeat or self-undoing; troubles; secrets; sorrows; disappointments and troubles; accidents; psychic powers.

The chart of the planets (Figure 45, page 154) shows the different ways we relate to life. It is best used for questions such as "What planetary energy do I need in my life?" or "What planet causes me stress?" Other good questions are "What is the best planetary energy for me?" or "Which is the most challenging planetary energy for me?"

This chart is composed of the five inner visible planets and the two luminaries that most strongly affect our lives, the three outer invisible planets, and Chiron, which is now being used more and more by astrologers. The five inner visible planets are Mercury, Venus, Mars, Jupiter, and Saturn, while the two luminaries are the Sun and the Moon. These seven "planets" were known and used by ancient astrologers long before there were telescopes to prove their existence.

The three outer invisible planets are Uranus, Neptune, and Pluto. The three outer planets are fairly new in astrology, for Uranus was only discovered in 1781, Neptune in 1846, and Pluto in 1930.

Chiron (pronounced Kyron) has an orbit between Saturn and Uranus, but which also allows it sometimes to wander between Jupiter and Saturn. Charles T. Kowal of the Hale Observatories at Pasadena, California discovered it in 1977. Chiron is larger than any asteroid, yet smaller than a planet. Not certain how Chiron should be classified, astronomers coined the name "planetoid," which means "like a planet." Its orbit is elliptical and takes fifty years to complete. This planetoid is named after the Greek centaur Chiron.

The inner planets and luminaries directly affect the way we live our lives—our personalities, our thoughts and feelings, our energies, our relationships, and the way we react to happenings around us. The outer planets affect less tangible aspects of life—our willingness and resolution to break from the past and create new paths, our awareness and sensitivity to the psychic and spiritual, and our ability to ride through transformations and begin renewals.

The chart of the planets is best used for certain kinds of questions such as:

"How can I deal with my parents?"
"What will occur if I make a specific change?"
"How should I handle a problem (name it)?"

Because it is possible for you to respond to any given situation in more than one way, it is best to dowse this chart at least twice, if not more times. This will show you all the possible ways you can use your individual energies and personality.

*Sun:* your outer personality; the individuality you show to the world; your active, energetic side; the conscious mind; will.

*Moon:* your inner personality; the side you rarely show to the world; the reflective, more emotional side; past conditioning that affects all your thoughts; the subconscious mind; the emotions; sensitivity; spontaneity; hidden personality.

*Mercury:* the mind and conscious thought; messages or messenger; the way you communicate; intelligence; perception; speech; memory; sarcasm; deceit; coldness.

*Venus:* the energy you give or demand in love; creative ability; your ability to love at all; happiness; indulgence; the arts; harmony; sensuality.

*Mars:* your assertiveness or lack of it; the will power and drive you possess; your energy in general; wants and desires; drive; initiative; courage; violence; selfishness; aggression.

*Jupiter:* good fortune; expansion; abundance; wisdom; success; overconfidence; extravagance; ethics; opportunity; faith; understanding; higher education; philosophy; overbearing; luck; morals; optimism.

*Saturn:* restrictions and self-limitations; the way you handle responsibility; your commitment to any person or goal; tests and lessons; fear; force of circumstances; discipline; limitations; order; obstacles; authority conflicts; time; ambition; material status; work; doubt; repression; responsibility; pessimism.

*Chiron:* the Wounded Healer; ancestral heritage; the black sheep or outsider; release and expansion; healing in a personal and universal sense; self-discovery; the inner teacher; our contribution to life; finding one's purpose in life.

*Uranus:* radical and sudden changes; the intuition; the degree to which you may or may not separate yourself from others; change; originality; upheaval; revolution; inventive; independence; unconventional turn of mind; disruption; unique; groups; unexpected; erratic; truth; reform; science; metaphysics; astrology; chaos; outsiders.

*Neptune:* spiritual; mysterious; mystical; psychic; delusions; sensitivity; escape; victim; compassion; suffering; healing; drugs; alcohol; fantasy; dissolving; confusing; imagination; artistic; visionary; clairvoyant.

*Pluto:* transformation; illumination; confrontation; regenerative forces; destruction; destiny; obsession; hidden things; birth and rebirth; insight; empowering; inner truth.

Burning incense many times will change the vibrations and atmosphere of a room or house. In many ways this is similar to the art of aromatherapy. Use the incense fan charts (Figures 46a–46b, pages 155–156) to determine which incense will be best for you at any given time and for any given problem. Often the immediate personal environment becomes contaminated with negative vibrations, whether from interaction of the people living there or by negative-minded people who visit. After dowsing with the pendulum for an incense, read the following descriptions to further clarify what may be happening and why this incense would help. Remember to use the Yes/No indicator to help you get through the charts more quickly.

*Cedar:* purification of an environment; repels evil spirits; associated with the summer solstice.
*Cinnamon:* protection;  healing; prosperity; stimulates clairvoyance.
*Frankincense:* protection; purification; exorcism; raises vibrations.
*Jasmine:* love; prosperity.
*Juniper:* protection, especially from accidents; repels thieves; attracts a lover.

*Lavender:* purification; protection; love; helps to reveal ghosts; aids in sleep.

*Lemon:* purification; aids in prophecy and divination.

*Lotus:* fertility; visions; helps with magic.

*Myrrh:* protection; purification; blesses an environment; helps with exorcisms.

*Patchouli:* attracts love and passion; protection; aids in clairvoyance and divination.

*Rose:* attracts love; fertility; clairvoyance; aids sleep.

*Sage:* purification; healing; prosperity.

*Sandalwood:* removes fears; protection; purification of an atmosphere; healing.

*Sweetgrass:* purification; brings blessings.

The gemstone chart is divided into seven charts for greater ease in divining (Figures 47a–47g, pages 157–163). Use these charts when you need to know what gemstones to wear or carry with you on an occasion. Wearing or carrying certain stones will add their vibration to your own vibrations, either strengthening what you need to face an event or adding a vibration in which you may be temporarily deficient. Remember to use the Yes/No indicator to help you get through the charts more quickly.

*Agate:* grounding; strengthening the mind and body; discovering the truth; protection.

*Amazonite:* soothes the nerves; aligns the mental and spiritual bodies; creative inspiration.

*Amber:* discovering past lives; calms fears; clears mental confusion.

*Amethyst:* promotes dreams; attracts good fortune; brings justice in court cases.

*Apache Tear:* channels higher beings and spirit guides.

*Aquamarine:* clears the mind; promotes creativity; banishes fear; balances the emotions and brings calmness.

*Aventurine:* releases anxieties; balances and calms; protection.

*Bloodstone:* guards against deceptions and cheating; prosperity; self-confidence.

*Carnelian:* speeds manifestation of desires; aligns the physical, mental, emotional, and spiritual bodies.

*Chrysoberl:* increases psychic awareness; strengthens the memory; prevents psychic manipulation by others.

*Chrysocolla:* clears away fears, guilt, and tensions; helps in dealing with anger connected with abuse; enhances creativity.

*Chrysoprase:* attracts prosperity; breaks negative habit patterns; calms the nerves.

*Citrine:* raises the self-esteem; protects the aura from negative influences; helps in dealing with karmic events.

*Coral:* calms the emotions; repels negative thoughts from others.

*Diamond:* helps to align the thoughts with the Higher Self; courage; victory.

*Emerald:* attracts prosperity; wards off negatives; enhances dreams and meditations.

*Flint:* helps survivors recover from abuse.

*Fluorite:* increases concentration; cleanses the aura; transformation.

*Fossil Wood:* attracts good luck; screens out negatives; eases stress.

*Garnet:* lifts depression; brings business opportunities; prevents nightmares.

*Iolite:* strengthens self-confidence; attracts friends.

*Jade:* increases fertility in all areas; balances the emotions; calms.

*Jasper:* protects and grounds; use for long-term changes.

*Labradorite:* stimulates physical energy and activity; protects and balances.

*Lapis Lazuli:* releases tension and anxiety; balances all the chakras; attracts a better job.

*Malachite:* repels evil spirits and accidents; helps with sleep; balances and heals all the chakras.

*Meteorite:* reveals past lives; expands the awareness.

*Moonstone:* helps to contact spiritual teachers; opens the psychic abilities.

*Obsidian:* grounds spiritual energy; protects; clears subconscious blockages.

*Onyx:* balances the emotions; self-control; helps in resolving past life problems.

*Opal:* enhances the intuition; balances the emotions; connects with the higher realms.

*Pearl:* balances and heals all the chakras; helps in the search for higher wisdom and truth; absorbs negatives.

*Peridot:* reduces stress; stimulates the mind; opens doors to opportunities.

*Pyrite:* increases self-esteem; harmonizes relationships; strengthens the will.

*Clear Quartz:* stimulates thinking; balances and harmonizes; repels negatives; enhances communications with the spirit world; helps with psychic powers.

*Rose Quartz:* heals emotional wounds; releases negative emotions; breaks up blockages; brings love.

*Smoky Quartz:* grounds and centers; breaks up subconscious blockages; strengthens dream messages; absorbs negatives.

*Ruby:* removes limitations; spiritual love; wisdom; stabilizes.

*Sapphire:* wards off poverty; breaks up confusion and blockages; aids in developing psychic powers.

*Sodalite:* calms and clears the mind; cuts through illusions; creates inner harmony.

*Sugilite:* balances and heals all the chakras; opens the mind to higher influences.

*Tanzanite:* mellows out extremes in a personality; calms and balances emotions.

*Tiger's Eye:* strengthens personal power; brings good luck; balances the emotions.

*Topaz:* dispels nightmares; repels depression and negative influences; prevents accidents.

*Black Tourmaline:* processes information from past lives; releases deeply buried negative emotions.

*Green Tourmaline:* regenerates; attracts prosperity; inspires creative ideas.

*Watermelon Tourmaline:* removes imbalances and guilt; helps to solve problems.

*Turquoise:* a master healer stone; enhances meditation; brings emotional balance; protects; helps to discover answers to life problems.

*Zircon:* brings peace with oneself; creates unity with spiritual teachers.

Many people have become familiar with the Native American concept of totem animals and want to know how to use them in their daily life. Others are aware that the Celts practiced a form of shamanism that incorporated animal allies. The charts for animal allies and totem animals, of which there are six (Figures 48a–48f, pages 164–169), can help you determine which animals you should focus on in order to attract certain animal characteristics. These characteristics are blended into the human aura for a brief period of time to help one cope with a troublesome situation or to aid in bringing the auric vibrations back into balance. Remember to use the Yes/No indicator to help you get through the charts more quickly.

*Ant:* orderliness; diligent work; planning; stamina; determination.

*Antelope:* learning to be aware when faced with new circumstances; recognizing and listening to your survival instincts.

*Badger:* standing up for your rights; learning when to release and when to control anger.

*Bat:* avoiding obstacles and negative people; leaping barriers; seeing the patterns in your past lives that influence this life.

*Bear:* strength; stamina; harmony in the family and life; listening to dreams.

*Bee:* planning for the future; prosperity; understanding reincarnation.

*Boar:* learning to stand up for yourself; defeating danger; protection.

*Buffalo/Bison:* working with spirit forces to accomplish goals; establishing a family; abundance; courage.

*Bull:* fertility; strength; abundance; protection.

*Butterfly:* reincarnation and rebirth; love; transformation.

*Cat:* recognizing when to fight and when to retreat; developing independence.

*Coyote:* recognizing and grasping opportunities; unveiling tricksters.

*Crow:* boldness and cunning when faced with enemies; keeping your eyes on your goal; releases painful past memories.

*Deer:* being alert to danger; developing poise and grace; abundance; learning from dreams; psychic abilities.

*Dog:* breaking through illusions to the truth; finding companionship; protection.

*Dolphin/Porpoise:* freedom; eloquence; changes; discover the truth; learning to communicate; harmony; creating balance in your life.

*Dragon:* protection; transformation of your life; spiritual knowledge.

*Dragonfly:* visions; mystical messages through dreams; breaking down illusions so the truth may be seen.

*Eagle:* strength; courage; wisdom; fearlessness in the face of great odds; discovering the overall pattern of your life and spiritual growth.

*Elk:* strength; stamina; learning to pace yourself in a job.

*Falcon:* healing; coming to terms with death; learning magic.

*Fox:* stealth; wisdom; cunning; masking your intentions when dealing with troublesome people.

*Frog:* initiations and transformations; dispelling negative vibrations; a new cycle in life.

*Hare, Rabbit:* transformation; quick thinking; learning to stop worrying.

*Hawk:* recalling past lives; being observant; overcoming problems; making decisions.

*Horse:* freedom; friendship and cooperation; taking journeys.

*Lizard:* facing and defeating your fears; learning spiritual knowledge from dreams and astral travel; handling difficult situations.

*Lynx:* developing divination skills and the psychic senses; understanding mystical secrets; looking within yourself and facing the truth.

*Mouse:* developing the ability to remain inconspicuous when necessary; watching for small details when signing contracts.

*Otter:* recovering from a crisis; enjoying life; learning to trust.

*Owl:* seeing through illusion; guidance in matters of dreams and astral travel; discovering hidden truth and secrets.

*Porcupine/Hedgehog:* building protective barriers that discourage enemies.

*Raven:* learning divination techniques; transformation; wisdom; creating or dealing with a change in consciousness.

*Snake:* facing your fears; connecting with psychic energy and spiritual initiation.

*Spider:* creativity; new life; industrious; patiently waiting for opportunities; beginning a new project.

*Squirrel:* preparing for the future; moving to a higher level of consciousness.

*Swan:* understanding dream symbols; spiritual evolvement; development of the intuition; keeping a serene exterior while dealing with private turmoil.

*Turtle/Tortoise:* developing patience and perseverance; giving yourself permission to slow down and enjoy life.

*Unicorn:* building individual power; gaining wisdom that will lead to success.

*Weasel:* using cunning, stealth, and ingenuity to overcome enemies.

*Whale:* developing positive relationships with your family and friends; learning psychic abilities.

*Wolf:* escaping dangerous enemies; outwitting enemies; learning from dreams; transformation.

Learning to use the pendulum in an effective manner can take you years, but these years will be filled with the excitement of learning more about yourself, your subconscious mind, your intuition, and the subtle effects of all these on your everyday life. Pendulum dowsing will open inner doors to greater psychic abilities, frequently enabling you to recall and use talents out of past lives. The truthfulness of your pendulum will depend upon your determination to see the truth, no matter how painful it may be at that moment. There is no greater experience than truth, for it sets us free of past and present shackles that hinder our spiritual growth. The pendulum can help you to become all you should have been and still can be.

# PENDULUM ILLUSTRATIONS

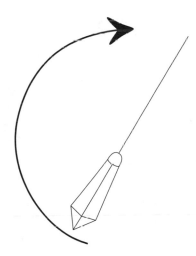

**Figure 1**
Clockwise Circles

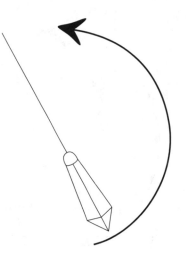

**Figure 2**
Counterclockwise Circles

**Figure 3**
Forward and Backward Movements

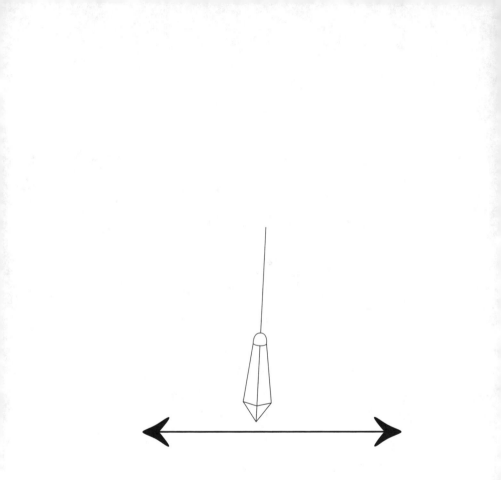

**Figure 4**
Side-to-Side Movements

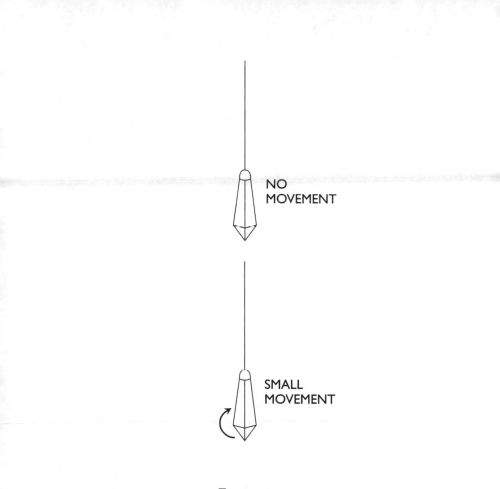

**Figure 5**
Neutral/Search Position

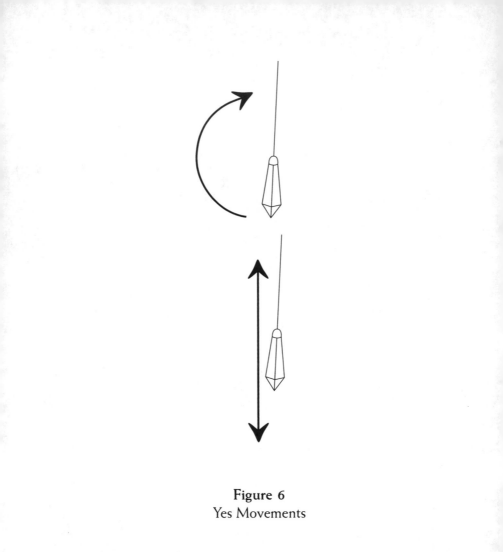

**Figure 6**
Yes Movements

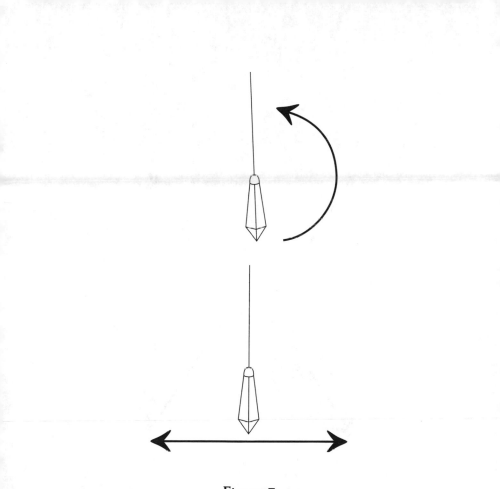

**Figure 7**
No Movements

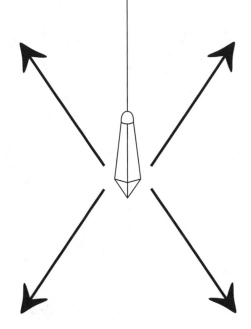

**Figure 8**
Confusion/Wrong Question Movements

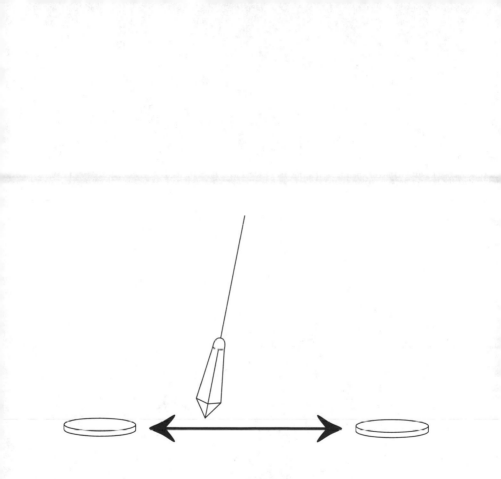

**Figure 9**
Two Coins Exercise

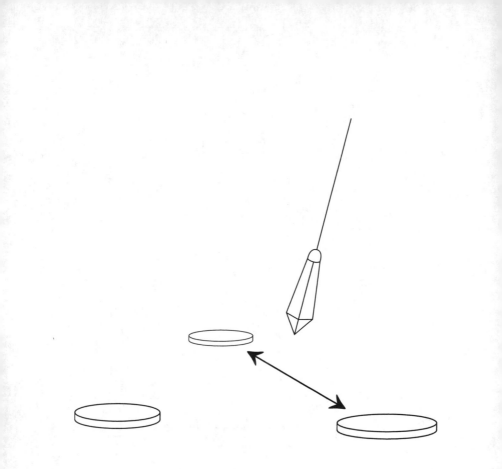

**Figure 10**
Three Coins Exercise

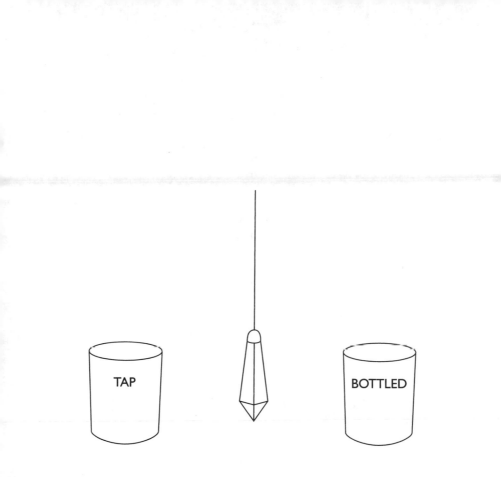

**Figure 11**
Two Glasses Exercise

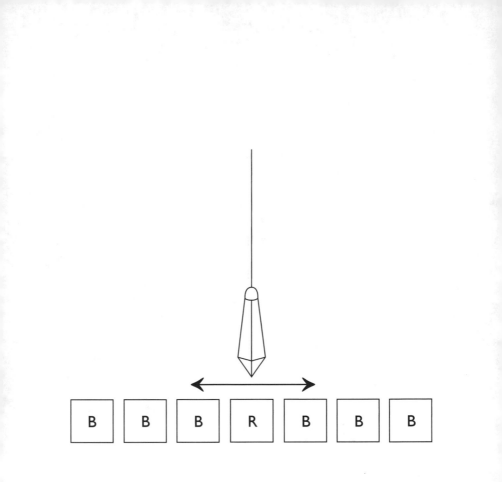

**Figure 12**
Red and Black Cards

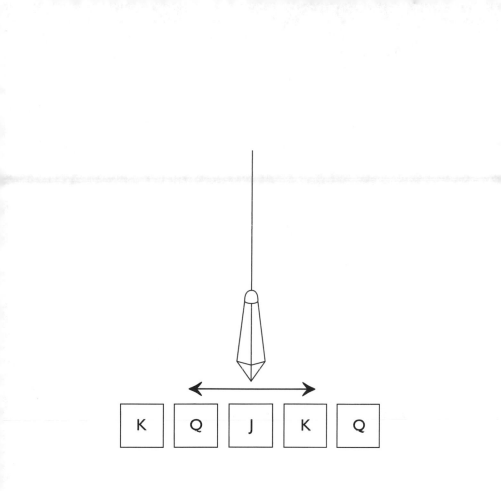

**Figure 13**
Face Cards

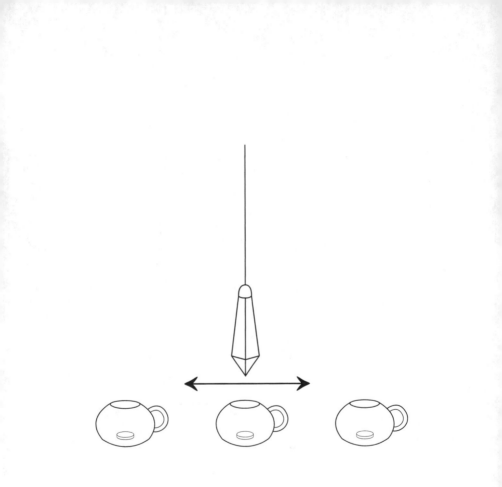

**Figure 14**
Three Objects

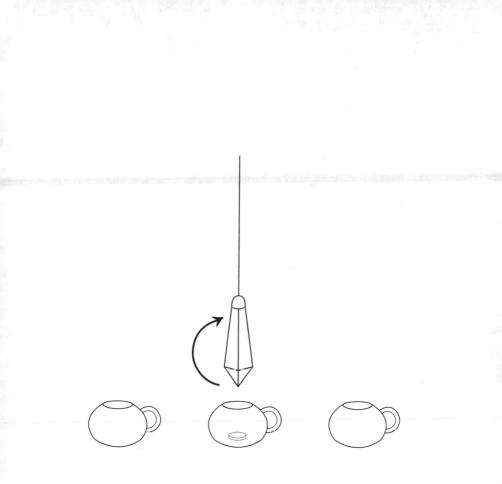

**Figure 15**
Three Cups and One Coin

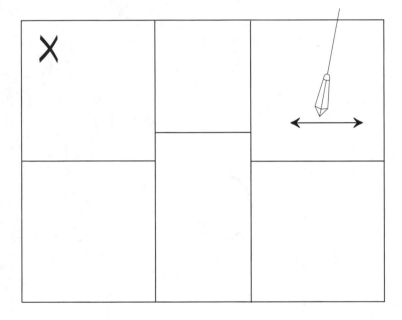

**Figure 16**
Finding an Object in a House

**Figure 17**
Nine Tarot Cards

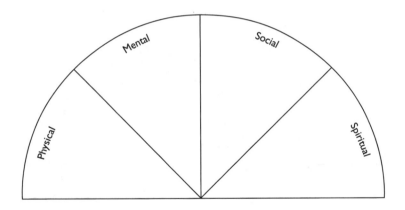

**Figure 18**
Realms of Life Chart

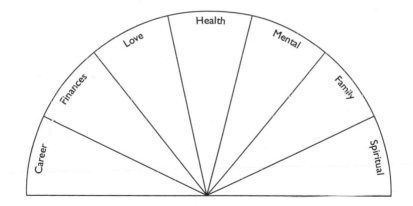

**Figure 19**
Life Areas Chart

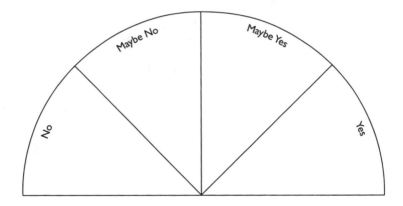

**Figure 20**
Yes/No/Maybe Chart

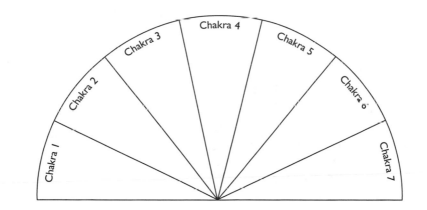

**Figure 21a**
The Chakras Chart

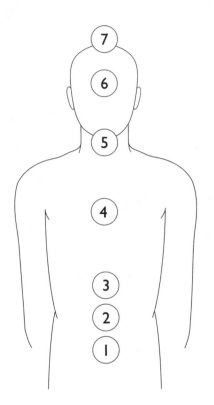

**Figure 21b**
Chakra Positions

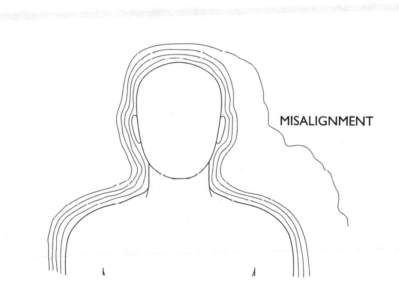

MISALIGNMENT

**Figure 22**
The Four Bodies

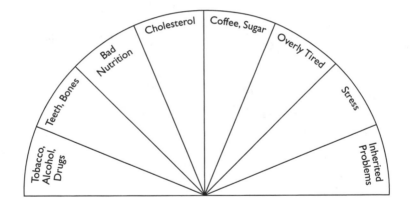

**Figure 23**
Physical Cause of Disease Chart

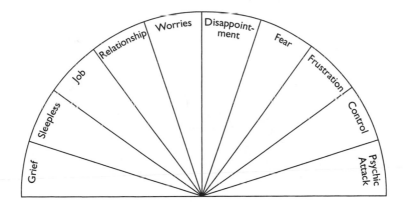

**Figure 24**
Psychic Cause of Disease Chart

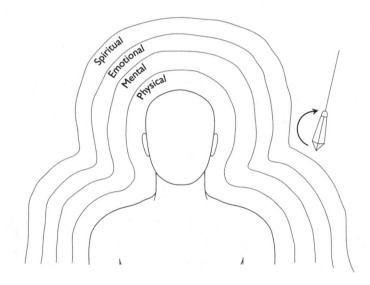

**Figure 25**
Auras

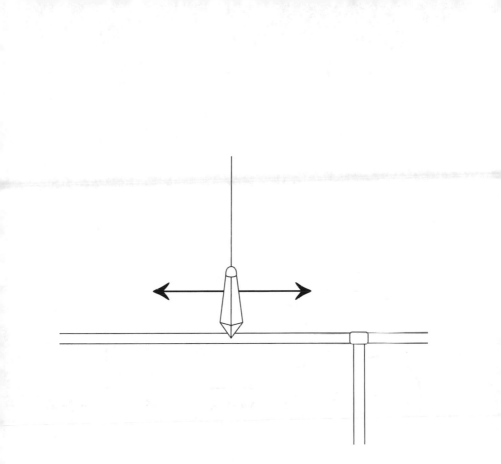

**Figure 26**
Finding Underground Lines

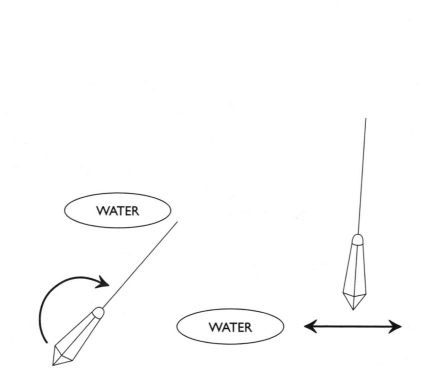

**Figure 27**
The Leading Edge Swing

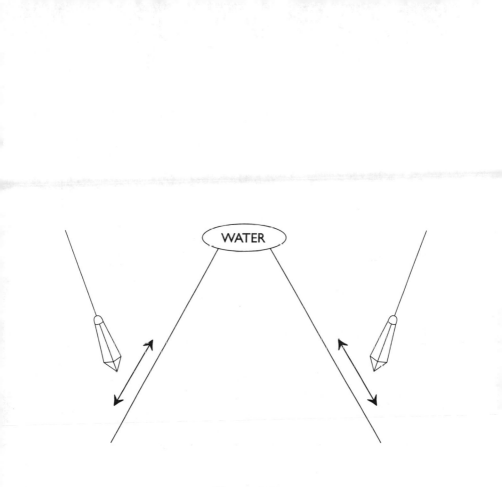

**Figure 28**
Triangulation

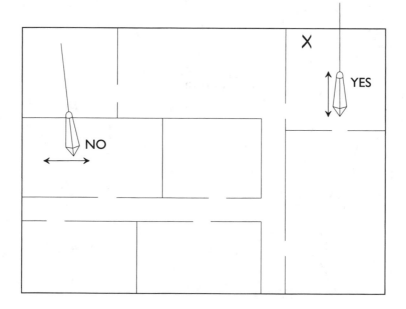

**Figure 29**
Floor Plan Dowsing

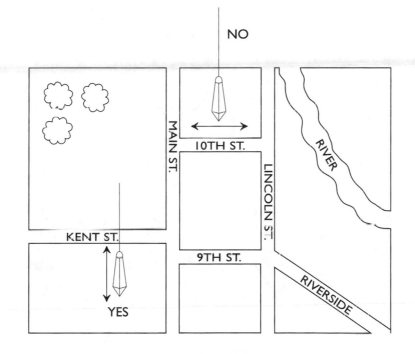

**Figure 30**
Map Dowsing

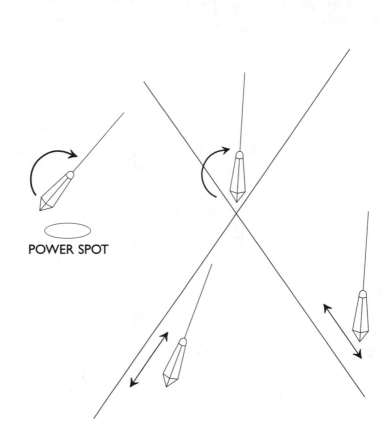

POWER SPOT

**Figure 31**
Dowsing Energy Lines

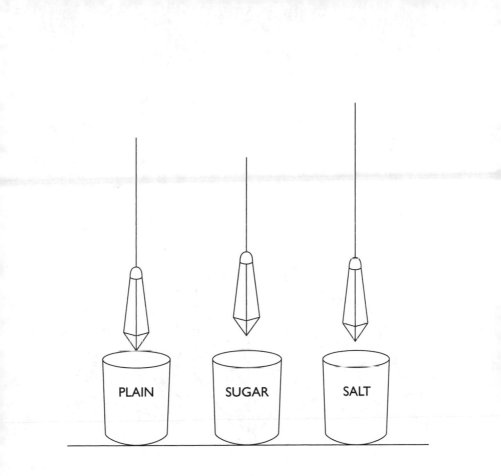

**Figure 32**
Three Glasses

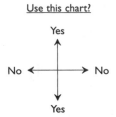

Use this chart?

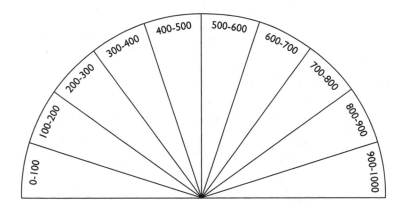

**Figure 33a**
Past Life Dates Chart

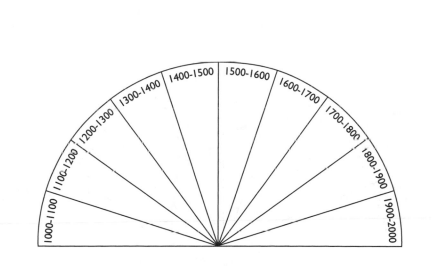

**Figure 33b**
Past Life Dates Chart

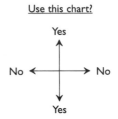

Use this chart?

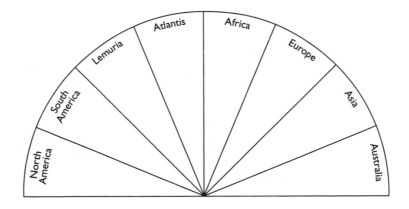

**Figure 34a**
Past Life Location Periods Chart

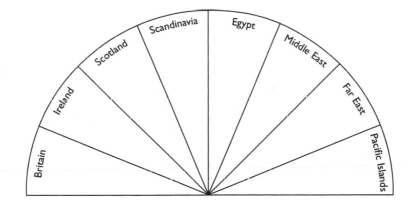

**Figure 34b**
Past Life Location Periods Chart

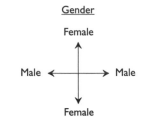

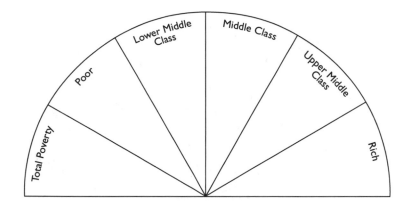

**Figure 35**
Past Life Social Background Chart

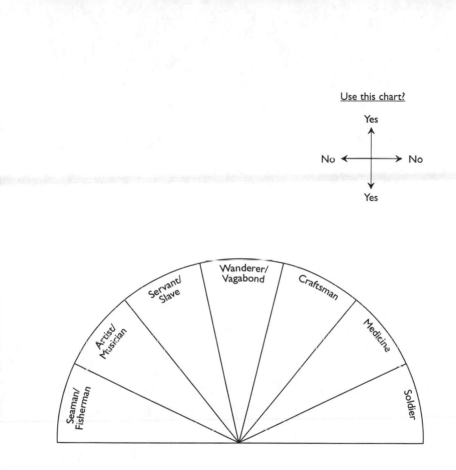

**Figure 36a**
Past Life Occupation Chart

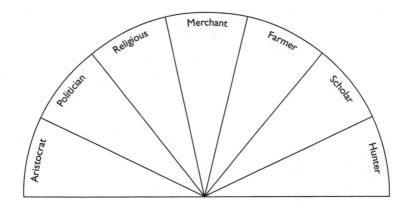

**Figure 36b**
Past Life Occupation Chart

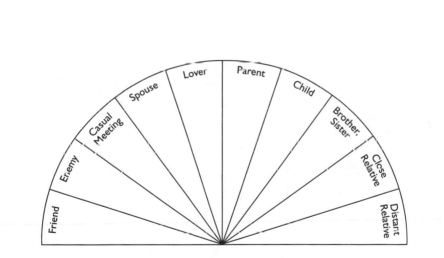

**Figure 37**
Past Life Karmic Relationships Chart

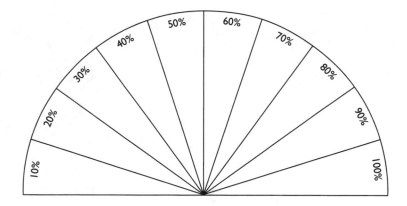

**Figure 38**
Accuracy Chart

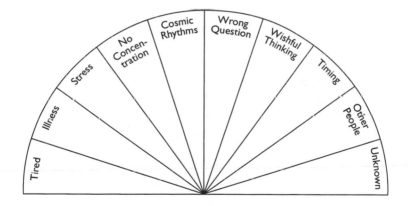

**Figure 39**
Inaccuracy Cause Chart

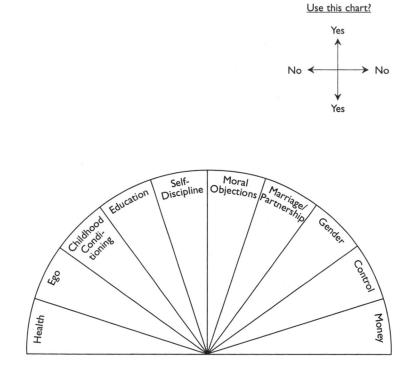

**Figure 40**
Obstacles (1) Chart

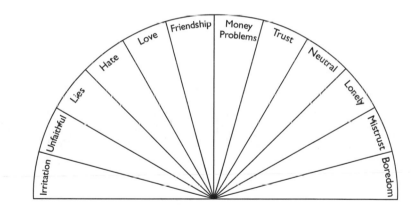

**Figure 41**
Obstacles (2) Chart

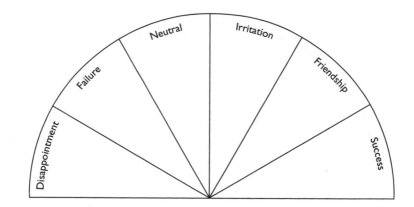

**Figure 42**
Destiny Chart

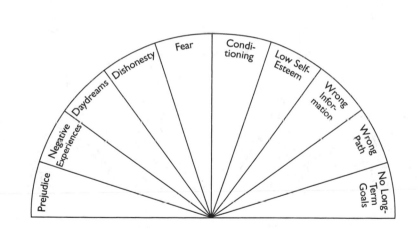

**Figure 43**
Blockages Chart

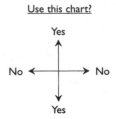

Use this chart?

Yes

No ← → No

Yes

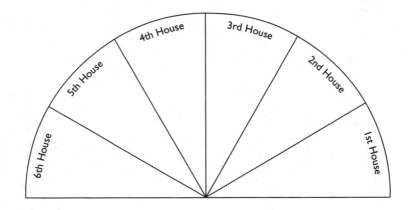

**Figure 44a**
Astrological Houses Chart

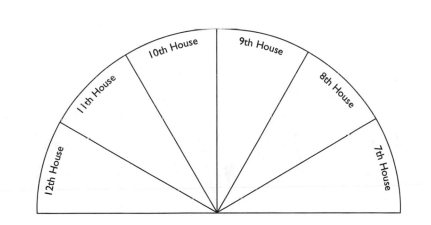

**Figure 44b**
Astrological Houses Chart

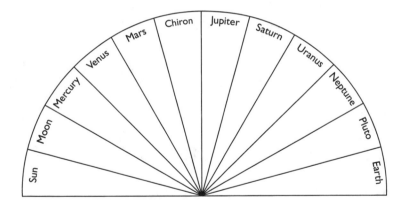

**Figure 45**
Planets Chart

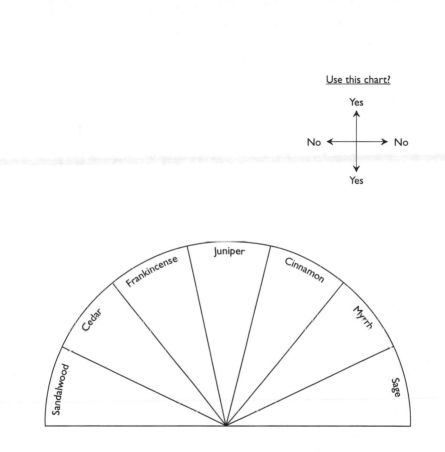

**Figure 46a**
Incense and Aromatherapy Chart

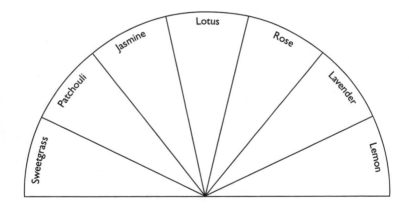

**Figure 46b**
Incense and Aromatherapy Chart

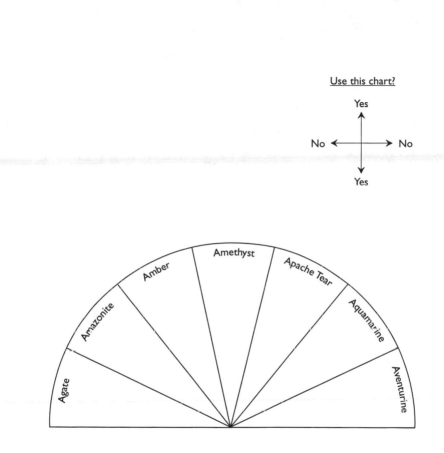

**Figure 47a**
Gemstones Chart

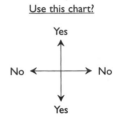

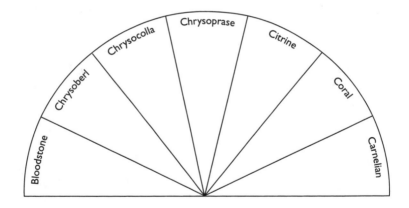

**Figure 47b**
Gemstones Chart

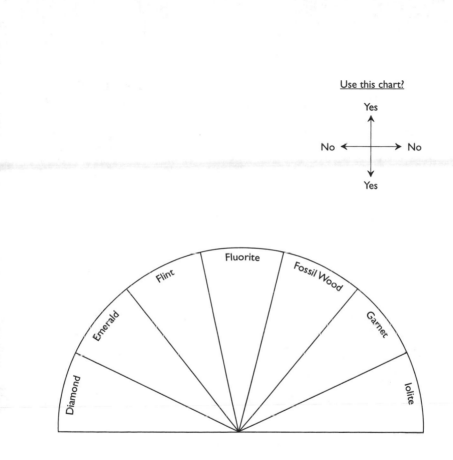

**Figure 47c**
Gemstones Chart

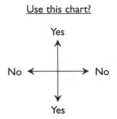

Use this chart?

Yes

No ← → No

Yes

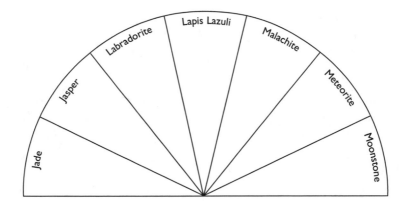

**Figure 47d**
Gemstones Chart

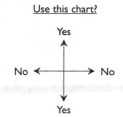

Use this chart?

Yes

No ← → No

Yes

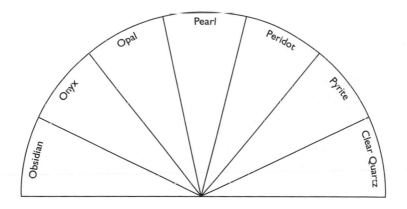

**Figure 47e**
Gemstones Chart

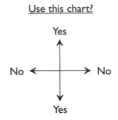

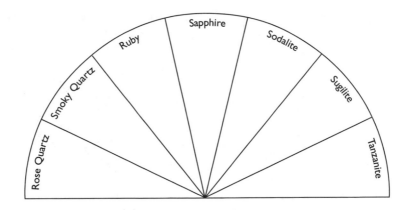

**Figure 47f**
Gemstones Chart

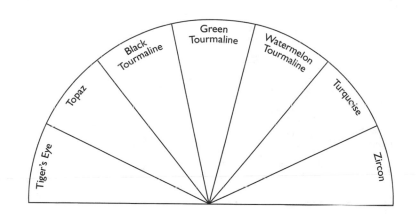

**Figure 47g**
Gemstones Chart

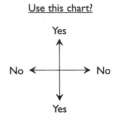

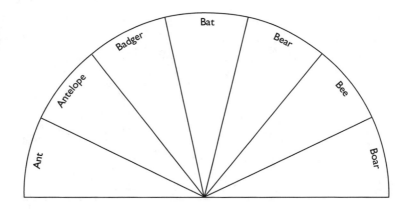

**Figure 48a**
Animal Allies or Totems Chart

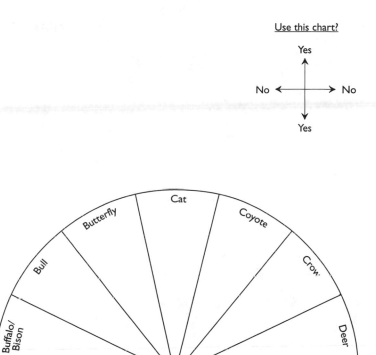

Use this chart?

Yes

No ← → No

Yes

Cat

Butterfly

Coyote

Bull

Crow

Buffalo/
Bison

Deer

**Figure 48b**
Animal Allies or Totems Chart

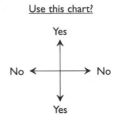

Use this chart?

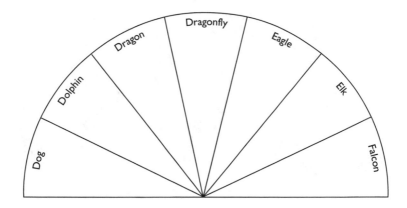

**Figure 48c**
Animal Allies or Totems Chart

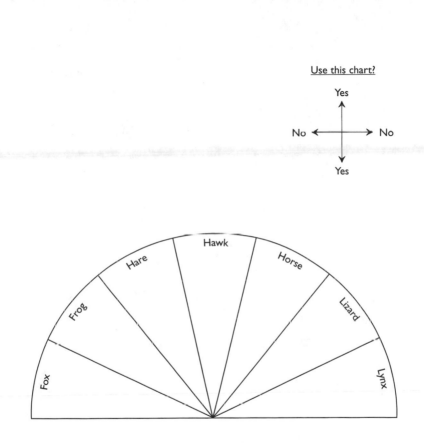

**Figure 48d**
Animal Allies or Totems Chart

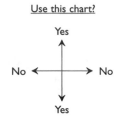

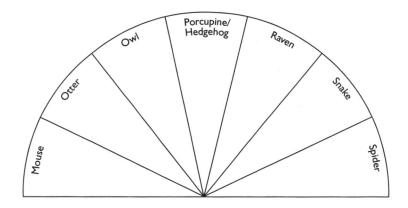

**Figure 48e**
Animal Allies or Totems Chart

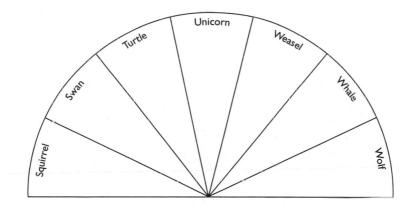

**Figure 48f**
Animal Allies or Totems Chart

# Bibliography

Bentov, Itzhak. *Stalking the Wild Pendulum: On the Mechanics of Consciousness*. Rochester, VT: Destiny Books, 1988. (Scientific and psychological studies of the pendulum.)

Bird, Christopher. *The Divining Hand*. NY: E. P. Dutton, 1979. (History of dowsing in the last five hundred years.)

Chandu, Jack F. *The Pendulum Book*. Translated by Tony Langham & Plym Peters. UK: C. W. Daniel Company, 1990.

Davies, Rodney. *Dowsing*. UK: The Aquarian Press, 1991.

de France, Le Vicomte Henry. *The Elements of Dowsing*. UK: G. Bell and Sons, 1948.

Finch, W. J. *The Pendulum & Possession*. Cottonwood, AZ: Esoteric Publications, 1975. (A good book if you totally ignore the propaganda about possession.)

Finch, Elizabeth & Bill. *The Pendulum and Your Health*. Cottonwood, AZ: Esoteric Publications, 1980.

Graves, Tom. *The Diviner's Handbook*. UK: The Aquarian Press, 1986.

Graves, Tom. *The Dowser's Workbook: Understanding & Using the Power of Dowsing*. NY: Sterling Publishing, 1990.

Graves, Tom. *Dowsing Techniques and Applications*. UK: Turnstone Books, 1976.

Graves, Tom. *The Elements of Pendulum Dowsing*. UK: Element Books, 1998.

Hitching, Francis. *Pendulum: The Psi Connection*. UK: Fontana, 1977.

Jurriaanse, D. *The Practical Pendulum Book*. NY: Samuel Weiser, 1986.

Lethbridge, T. C. *The Power of the Pendulum*. NY: Routledge & Kegan Paul, 1976.

Lethbridge, Tom. *Ghost and Divining Rod*. UK: Routledge & Kegan Paul, 1963. (Ghost hunting with the dowsing rod and pendulum.)

Lonegren, Sig. *Earth Mysteries*. Danville, VT: ASD Book & Supply, 1985. (Sacred geometry, archaeoastronomy, and dowsing.)

Lonegren, Sig. *The Pendulum Kit*. NY: Simon & Schuster, 1990.

Lonegren, Sig. *Spiritual Dowsing*. UK: Gothic Image Publications, 1986. (Earth energies, sacred sites, healing.)

Nielsen, Greg. *Beyond Pendulum Power*. Reno, NV: Conscious Books, 1988.

Nielsen, Greg and Joseph Polansky. *Pendulum Power*. Rochester, VT: Destiny Books, 1987.

Powell, Tag & Judith. *Taming the Wild Pendulum*. Pinellas Park, FL: Top of the Mountain Publishing, 1995.

Schirner, Mark. *Pendulum Workbook*. NY: Sterling Publishing, 1999.

Scott-Elliott, Major General James. *Dowsing—One Man's Way*. UK: Neville Spearman, 1977.

Underwood, Guy. *The Pattern of the Past*. NY: Abelard-Schuman, 1973. (Advanced earth energy dowsing.)

Underwood, Peter. *The Complete Book of Dowsing & Divining*. UK: Rider & Company, 1980.

Weaver, Herbert. *Divining, the Primary Sense*. UK: Routledge & Kegan Paul, 1978.

Webster, Richard. *Dowsing for Beginners*. St. Paul, MN: Llewellyn Publications, 1996.

# Other Books by D. J. Conway

## Advanced Celtic Shamanism

"You do not have to be of Celtic lineage to benefit from the teaching of this book. You only need a sincere desire to better yourself, patience to work your way through the paths, and a positive attitude. If you are lacking the positive attitude at this time, be assured that it will come through your efforts and Otherworld journeys." *from the Introduction*

Paper • ISBN-13: 978-1-58091-073-6 / ISBN-10: 1-58091-073-4

## Crystal Enchantments: A Complete Guide to Stones and Their Magical Properties

D. J. Conway's book will help guide you in your choice of stones from Adularia to Zircon, by listing their physical properties and magical uses. It will also appeal to folks who are not into magic, but simply love stones and want to know more about them.

Paper • ISBN-13: 978-1-58091-010-1 / ISBN-10: 1-58091-010-6

## Laying on of Stones

Stones can be used to protect and heal you, your family, and your home, but where to place them is often a source of difficulty. Probably the most important question frequently asked is where to place them on your body. D. J. Conway has supplied you with forty detailed diagrams, showing you exactly how to place a variety of stones to help your body heal itself of illness or enrich your life through a magical manifestation of desires.

Paper • ISBN-13: 978-1-58091-029-3 / ISBN-10: 1-58091-029-7

# Other Books in the Series

## Little Book of Altar Magic

By D. J. Conway

Read this book, set your altar, and take control of your life. Setting up an altar makes us receptive to the sacred. It requires clarifying the reasons for making the altar, choosing where to build it, and what to include. An altar created with such intent can help make your life richer and also attract into your life what you wish to find.

Paper • ISBN-13: 978-1-58091-052-1 / ISBN-10: 1-58091-052-1

## Little Book of Candle Magic

By D. J. Conway

This book explains the purpose of ritual, how to play with candles and colors, and how to perform candle spells. The use of incense, oil, herbs, stones, and the timing of rituals by the moon and days of the year is also explained. Prairie Wind Stock says about Little Book of Candle Magic, "I highly recommend this book—these spells really work!"

Paper • ISBN-13: 978-1-58091-043-9 / ISBN-10: 1-58091-043-2

## A Little Book of Love Magic

By Patricia Telesco

A cornucopia of lore, magic, and imaginative ritual designed to bring excitement and romance to your life. Patricia Telesco tells us how to use magic to manifest our hopes and dreams for romantic relationships, friendships, family relations, and passions for our work.

Paper • ISBN-13: 978-0-89594-887-8 / ISBN-10: 0-89594-887-7

### Aromatherapy: A Complete Guide to the Healing Art

By Kathi Keville and Mindy Green

This complete guide presents everything you need to know to enhance your health, beauty, and emotional well-being through the practice of aromatherapy. Kathi Keville and Mindy Green offer a fresh perspective on the most fragrant of the healing arts.

Paper • ISBN-13: 978-0-89594-692-8 / ISBN-10: 0-89594-692-0

### Color and Crystals: A Journey Through the Chakras

By Joy Gardner-Gordon

Information about color, crystals, tones, personality types, and Tarot archetypes that correspond to each chakra. Fully illustrated, indexed and well-organized.

Paper • ISBN-13: 978-0-89594-258-6 / ISBN-10: 0-89594-258-5

### Spinning Spells, Weaving Wonders: Modern Magic for Everyday Life

By Patricia Telesco

This essential book of over 300 spells tells how to work with simple, easy-to-find components and focus creative energy to meet daily challenges with awareness, confidence, and humor.

Paper • ISBN-13: 978-0-89594-803-8 / ISBN-10: 0-89594-803-6

✳

For a current catalog of books from Crossing Press visit our Web site at: **www.tenspeed.com**.